Edith Wharton and the Novel of Manners

Edith Wharton
and
the Novel of Manners

Gary H. Lindberg

University Press of Virginia
Charlottesville

THE UNIVERSITY PRESS OF VIRGINIA
Copyright © 1975 by the Rector and Visitors
of the University of Virginia

First published 1975

Library of Congress Cataloging in Publications Data

Lindberg, Gary H   1941-
    Edith Wharton and the novel of manners.

    Bibliography: p.
    Includes index.
    1. Wharton, Edith Newbold Jones, 1862-1937—Criticism and
interpretation.   I. Title.   PS3545.H16Z698   813'.5'2   75-17504
ISBN 0-8139-0563-X

Printed in the United States of America

Acknowledgments

Claude M. Simpson, Jr., and Thomas C. Moser read an early version of the manuscript and not only gave me important practical suggestions but offered the kind of encouragement that keeps one happily at work. R. W. B. Lewis made clear to me the basis for my revisions at a later stage of the manuscript. I am deeply grateful to these men for their help, and I am especially grateful to David Levin, who had the patience to read each version of the manuscript, the acuteness to catch both stylistic blunders and flaws of argument, and the kindness to make me return for his judgments. During more casual talk with friends, of course, one's possible paths of thought are lighted up and one's questions affirmed as genuine or discarded as needing no answer. Two people have been particularly important in this subtler shaping of my ideas here, Anthony Winner, for matters involving the novel of manners, and Alan Howard, for matters related to American literature. The University of Virginia Faculty Fellowships for Summer Research supported me during my most concentrated work on the manuscript. Finally, I wish to thank Charles Scribner's Sons for permission to quote from Edith Wharton's *The Age of Innocence* and *A Backward Glance*.

Contents

Acknowledgments   v
Introduction   1

  I   The Individual in Society:
        Character and Personage   13

  II   The Mind in Chains:
        Public Plots and Personal Fables   43

  III   Manners in Narrative:
        The Emergence of Society   87

  IV   Characterization:
        Manners and Psychology   109

  V   Analytic Style:
        The Filtering of Judgment   140

  VI   The Ritualistic Social Scene:
        An Assessment   161

Bibliographical Essay   179
Index   185

Edith Wharton and the Novel of Manners

Introduction

In 1921 Vernon L. Parrington asked two disturbing questions about Edith Wharton's *The Age of Innocence:* "What do the van der Luydens matter to us: or what did they or their kind matter a generation ago? Why waste such skill upon such insignificant materials?" By now, of course, we all know that Edith Wharton was a novelist of manners, and with this convenient category in mind we could dismiss these questions as irrelevant. But to do so would be to dismiss her achievement, for Parrington's questions are serious and must be confronted directly. In the context of American suspicions about social class and social codes, the novel of manners is a problematic form, and no major American novelist—not even Cooper or James or Fitzgerald—has dealt with it so purely and so comprehensively as Wharton. In making "such insignificant materials" matter, she raises primary questions about the possibilities of the novel: what does it mean to be a novelist of manners? What is society?

These are hard questions because the novel of manners has been so familiar for so long that it has never received the critical scrutiny it deserves. There is no standard formulation of its makeup, its range, or its characteristic strategies. Defining the novel of manners generically involves difficulties like those one faces in defining the novel itself. The basic problem in both instances is that technical, structural, or formal qualifications inevitably narrow the focus too much, making it awkward to compare Jane Austen and Balzac as novelists of manners or, more extremely, to join Fielding and Robbe-Grillet as novelists. The logical art of definition depends on careful exclusion, and the exclusions by which the novel of manners or the novel might be determined will inevitably be prescriptive. The usefulness of a generic definition, on the other hand, turns less on exclusion than on emphasis—what kinds of things can this genre or medium do especially well? Let me begin with the novel and then turn specifically to the novel of manners. The emphasis in novels has to do both with form and with substance, or theme. Whatever the shortcomings of particular attempts to define the novel, one cannot help coming back to narrative, or storytelling, and to "realism." Without trying to recreate the full argumentative context in which one attempts to define the novel,[1] I will simply say that for me the most useful way of getting at the special emphasis in novels is to look at them as accounts of what happens when inadequate fictions are brought to bear on a denser, more substantial reality. The fictions to be tested and modified may range from outmoded social or literary conventions to personal wishes that do not account for the wills of others, but in each instance they exist as stories or story-fragments, aligning expectations and projecting desires in time. It is the anticipation created by such fictions that makes apparent the resisting density of the surrounding world, converting reality into experience, as Don Quixote's chivalric stories bring into prominence the details of life in sixteenth-century Spain. This approach to the novel acknowledges both the formal importance of narrative, with its shifts of experience in time, and the thematic importance of realism, of those treacherous particularities somehow left out of one's plans, one's hopes, and one's conventional accountings of experience.

Realism, however, is the concept that tends to make definitions of the novel too exclusive, for reality is easily assumed to be materialistic, bourgeois, and social. At the risk of open-endedness, I prefer to leave "reality" to the determination of the novelist.

---

[1] Among the major arguments about what novels are, all focusing on problems of realism, the following are especially helpful: Erich Auerbach, *Mimesis,* trans. Willard Trask (Princeton, 1953); Lionel Trilling, *The Liberal Imagination* (New York, 1950); Northrop Frye, *Anatomy of Criticism* (Princeton, 1957); Ian Watt, *The Rise of the Novel* (London, 1957); Harry Levin, *The Gates of Horn* (New York, 1963). See also Philip Stevick's anthology *The Theory of the Novel* (New York, 1967) and the ongoing theoretical discussions in the journal *Novel,* especially in the first three volumes. My own formulation combines features from Barbara Hardy, "Towards a Poetics of Fiction: An Approach through Narrative," *Novel,* 2 (Fall 1968), 5-14, and Maurice Z. Shroder, "The Novel as a Genre," *Massachusetts Review,* 4 (1963), 291-308. Shroder sees the process of the novel as "demythification," the generic equivalent of the protagonist's own experiential disillusionment. My approach is very close to his except in ranging beyond his emphasis on "an education into the realities of the material world and of human life in society."

Thus a Gothic fiction could still be examined as a novel; it exposes as inadequate the fiction that human nature is primarily rational and social, and it explores the dense particularity of dream, irrationality, unowned complicities, isolating impulses, and fear. In other words, I prefer to regard Fielding and Richardson, Jane Austen and Flaubert, Robbe-Grillet and Hawkes all as novelists, and then, by discriminating among the fictions they puncture and the denser realities they affirm, to distinguish their emphases.

This general strategy suggests a basis for clarifying the novel of manners. But first, what are manners themselves? Here one must frankly turn from literary to social concerns. Manners are those patterns of behavior that have their origins and their significance within a specific social order. They are real or implied actions—in gesture, speech, decoration, dress—that provide forms for individual expression, and *within* the social order these forms quicken public feelings by summoning up unspoken meanings and beliefs;[2] they make up, in Edith Wharton's phrase, "a kind of hieroglyphic world." The novel of manners, then, is a novel in which the dense, particular reality that resists the inadequate fiction is significantly made up of the conventions of one or more social orders. It will be seen that this definition says almost nothing about form or technique, beyond the implied reference to narrative; I do not feel that there are particular techniques or structures that determine the novel of manners. In contrast, the definition offers two kinds of flexibility. The first concerns those conventions or manners that are to be stressed. Jane Austen obviously finds verbal behavior far more important than any other mode of manners; for Balzac those patterns of behavior involving dress, decoration, and gesture assume relatively greater significance. This contrast, in turn, informs some of the basic technical differences in their fictions and suggests why Balzac was a more important influence on Edith Wharton than Austen was. But it does not make one more than the other a novelist of manners. The second kind of flexibility involves degree

---

[2]Compare Lionel Trilling's famous definition of manners as "a culture's hum and buzz of implication. I mean the whole evanescent context in which its explicit statements are made. It is that part of a culture which is made up of half-uttered or unuttered or unutterable expressions of value" (*The Liberal Imagination,* p. 206).

of emphasis. When is a novel's reality "significantly made up" of manners? There is no exact measure; it is a matter of the reader's tact. Edith Wharton's reality is far more dependent on manners than Howells's, and his more than Fitzgerald's; yet I would agree with the consensus that all three are novelists of manners. On the other hand, the definition does provide a framework within which it would make sense to argue, for example, about whether Fitzgerald *is* a novelist of manners, and that kind of sense is as much as one can reasonably ask of a working generic definition.

A misconception, however, is possible at this point. Given that the novelist believes his reality to be true and the characters' fictions to be inadequate, doesn't my definition imply that the novelist of manners believes social convention to be right and personal wishes to be wrong? The most general way of answering no here is to recall that a novelist need not *like* what he shows to be real, as in Cervantes's notorious mixture of feelings about Quixote's imagination and about what challenges it. When I say that reality in the novel of manners is significantly made up of social convention, I do not mean that manners are normative or that the social order is the arbiter of reality. I simply mean that in the novel of manners it is important that the character's fictions are inadequate, his expectations illusory, because they do not account for the importance of manners, whether as determiners of conduct, as separators of persons, or as bases of inadvertent exposure. Novels of manners show the relation between the individual and social convention to be more serious, more difficult, more dense and demanding than the central characters had expected. If the general concern of the novel is the conflict of fiction and substantiality, the particular area in which novels of manners reveal this conflict is the meeting place of the self and one or more sets of manners. The novel of manners may thus satirize certain conventions, showing their baleful or comic effects on particular persons, but it cannot, without shifting emphasis and becoming another genre, stress the irrelevance, emptiness, or unreality of manners themselves. Whatever more specific judgments it may suggest, the novel of manners takes the influence of manners seriously.

A brief survey of Edith Wharton's major subject matter will indicate both why the novel of manners was her inevitable mode and why society is so problematic and serious in her fiction. First, consider her historical subject. The social background against which Wharton projected her major fiction offered one of the richest fields in American history for the novelist of manners. Despite the steady movement of families and fortunes and despite the absence of a true aristocracy, the New York of her youth, in the years after the Civil War, was still socially dominated by a small class that nearly passed, among Americans, for an aristocracy, the class identified in her fiction with "old New York." A few families in this class actually traced their roots to the English or the Dutch aristocracies, but most were of "respectable mercantile stock"— that is, their wealth derived from wholesale trade, shipping, and real estate investment conducted in the eighteenth and early nineteenth centuries. Their fortunes were old enough, on the one hand, to seem part of the very nature of things and, on the other hand, to allow intervening generations to develop a relatively coherent set of manners and class ideals. The last third of the nineteenth century, however, also saw new fortunes accumulating, both in Wall Street and in "the West," at a rate meteoric by earlier standards. During these years a multitude of the newly enriched gravitated to New York as a field for both larger financial operations and social advancement.

Historically, the transfer of social power from the mercantile "aristocracy" to the modern industrial plutocracy occurred gradually over much of the last century and some of the present one. But after the Civil War the tempo changed significantly, and in Edith Wharton's condensation the 1880s form the essential period of cleavage between the two orders. This assumption of a cataclysmic change allows her to dramatize vividly what actually took place less perceptibly. In her summary this is what happened. Between the Civil War and the end of the nineteenth century, a horde of suddenly enriched "invaders" besieged and finally overran the "aboriginal" culture of old New York. Having had little time to develop manners cognate with their wealth, the invaders tried at first, and with limited success, to imitate the behavior and appearances of the aborigines. Later they disregarded what they could not understand, obscuring the quiet restraint of the older families in a blaze of social promiscuity that came to characterize New York after the turn of the century.

In this situation Wharton found all the outward signs the novel of manners analyzes: marked distinctions in behavior and class values, movement from one social milieu to another with its attendant personal confusions, imitation of manners and of objects to desire. She also encountered, especially in her later years, one of the gravest ironies of the novel of manners: that by the time it has analyzed a given set of manners, they have often changed from the vehicles of assumptions shared by author, character, and reader to quaint gestures in a long-since abandoned social ritual. At her best Wharton escapes this irony by using her analysis of the particular conventions of New York as the basis upon which to investigate the role of manners themselves in human affairs, and this problem motivates her finest fiction.

Second, let us consider the broader moral subject Wharton saw in this historical situation. When systems of behavior come into conflict, and especially when these systems represent groups immersed in historical change, the very ground of moral judgment begins to slip. By attaching its own significance to a given form of behavior, each class acts under a different sanction, and in time some of these meanings will be lost. The moral issues informing one person's judgments may be invisible or even repugnant to another. And behind these immediate sources of confusion lies the larger question faced by the novelist of manners: can we not judge conduct by reference to something that transcends local variations and changes in time? What is the relation of manners to morals? With her own moral seriousness and intelligence, such questions loomed large for Edith Wharton. For all her apparent exclusiveness, especially in the later novels, she was rarely beguiled into an unwitting equation of class index and moral principle. But precisely because she recognized the appeal of more than one system of judgment, the moral situation in her fiction is often perplexing.

The basis of the difficulty is that the local social order or class diverges from the larger society, culture, and tradition of which it ought to be a part. Wharton shows a profound admiration for continuity in human affairs—between human needs and social arrangements, between individual and class, between class and culture. She sees "all mortality's immortal gains" as arising from the cumulative efforts of human yearning; the concepts of beauty, truth, and goodness have emerged from traditional development.

In passages of authorial theorizing, Wharton affirms as her ideal a situation in which the moral intelligence deliberates to preserve this continuity; it harmonizes impulses, modulates personal needs by reference to the communal good, and reconciles the sanctions of the community itself with the values of the larger traditions in which it is grounded. But these passages of theory often diverge from the issues raised by the stories themselves. Her characters rarely get a clear enough grasp on themselves or their situations to deliberate effectively; the cleavage between private yearnings and public demands is so wide that her characters must renounce personal fulfillment; and all too often the customs of the immediate social order conflict with the larger sanctions and promises of the cultural tradition. What Henry James called her "infernal keenness of perception" forced Wharton to recognize that the actual effects of social organization do not match her deeper expectations.

"There are moments," Newland Archer muses, "when a man's imagination, so easily subdued to what it lives in, suddenly rises above its daily level, and surveys the long windings of destiny." But such moments are rare in Wharton's view, and for this reason the disparity between her ideals and her observations made local custom more, not less, important to her. Recognizing that the imagination is "easily subdued to what it lives in," she acknowledged the terrible difficulty of rising above the special outward circumstances of one's life, and she devoted the substance of her best fiction to an investigation of life at the "daily level."

There is a third, and still more general, way of regarding Edith Wharton's subject matter. In order to understand this divergence of ideal and actual or, more precisely, to make out the nature and significance of life at the daily level, Wharton turned to "the wonder-world of nineteenth century science," to cultural anthropology and early sociology and evolutionary studies. In her autobiography she stresses the importance of her readings in "the great evolutionary movement," trying to convey to younger readers "the first overwhelming sense of cosmic vastnesses which such 'magic casements' let into our little geocentric universe."[3] And it

---

[3] *A Backward Glance* (New York, 1964), p. 94. In describing these "magic casements," Wharton refers specifically to Darwin, Huxley, Herbert Spencer, Romanes, Haeckel, and Westermarck. For my brief summary of an anthropological account of moral ideas, I

is the perspective of evolutionary science and anthropology that provides the cool, distant intelligence one so often recognizes in Wharton's best fiction. One finds throughout her writings allusions to primitive tribes and evolutionary development. Far from ridiculing local behavior, these references suggest its awesome significance: "what was or was not 'the thing' played a part as important in Newland Archer's New York as the inscrutable totem terrors that had ruled the destinies of his forefathers thousands of years ago."[4] From the habits and questions of the anthropologist, Wharton derived a new comprehension of manners, morals, and society, and it is through the convergence of anthropology with the novel of manners that one most broadly understands her subject matter.

If Wharton's theoretical comments suggest that moral ideas arise in a long tradition of rational deliberation, cumulatively approaching the realm of absolute truth, the anthropological account of moral ideas differs critically. Sophisticated moral concepts appear as generalizations of primitive moral emotions—indignation or approval. Private and instinctive in themselves, these retributive emotions become public when powerful men impose their likes and dislikes on their fellows; and as soon as later generations forget the partiality of this procedure, the implicitly established rules of conduct become habitual and obligatory. The very idea of morality emerges in the public conjunction of tribal customs and primitive emotion. This account suggests both the frightening power of local manners on the psyche and the difficulty of employing rational deliberation in the personal case. When Wharton investigates the individual consciousness, she repeatedly begins by tracing the effects on it of local customs and public feelings, by showing the roots of the personality in the immediate social order. Following the model of comparative anthropology, she initiates her characters' moral growth toward more impartial reflection in the juxtaposition and comparison of conflicting customs. Even when a character cannot rise to genuinely impartial, clear insights, she deals seriously

---

have followed Edward Westermarck's *The Origin and Development of the Moral Ideas* (1906).

[4]*The Age of Innocence* (New York, 1920), p. 2. Subsequent references to this edition will appear in the text.

with the moral bewilderment accompanying exposure to new ways of behaving and judging.

The new concepts of anthropological and sociological inquiry affected Wharton's idea of society as strongly as they influenced her notions of manners and morals. Instead of the totality of relationships into which a collection of individuals can enter with each other, society emerges in her fiction as a living entity, larger than the sum of persons making it up and essentially independent of their individual qualities. One sees in such passages as the following her characteristic tendency to attribute to society volitions, powers, and subtleties not strictly arising from any of its particular members: "Society did not turn away from her, it simply drifted by, preoccupied and inattentive, letting her feel, to the full measure of her humbled pride, how completely she had been the creature of its favour."[5] And throughout *The Age of Innocence* old New York materializes as a tribal body with an instinctive perspicacity, a primitive power of self-preservation, that transcends the interests of any individual New Yorkers. The tribal allusions, then, pertain to a mode of analysis: Wharton investigates a society as an anthropologist examines a tribe, not as a collection of persons but as a system of sanctions, taboos, customs, and beliefs. This abstract system is, in turn, reified by both author and characters, assuming a personality that corresponds to the moral ambience of the community. Like a relic hunter piecing together fragments out of a Babylonian tomb, Wharton assumes that by assembling and labeling the particular manners and artifacts of a social order, she will be able to bring to life a corporate being of immense interest and importance—a way of life, a society.

This corporate being lies at the center of her curiosity as a novelist; she brings a nearly scientific zeal to her enumeration and analysis of local customs, her dramatization of a society's characteristic functions. Although this peculiar focus makes Edith Wharton sound primarily like a sociologist or a social historian, she brings to her fiction another set of commitments that quicken her imagination. Despite her ardent observation and analysis of life at the daily level, she remains deeply moved by the assumptions

---

[5]*The House of Mirth* (New York, 1905), p. 422. Subsequent references to this edition will appear in the text.

and values of traditional humanism—the dignity of man, the supreme importance of the individual soul, the ultimate accountability of human behavior and thought to a realm of absolute truth. When she dramatizes a social order, then, her chief means of assessing it is to measure its impact on individual beings, to explore the influence of a set of manners on the inward life of a substantial character. The question she asks is anthropological: what is the role of manners in human affairs? But the field in which she asks the question is novelistic; that is, it is dense, particular, biased toward the individual and the personal, resistant to easy theory and open to the illuminations of imagined experience.

It is in this sense that the novel of manners is so exacting a vehicle for Edith Wharton: its domain—the relation of the individual to one or more sets of manners—is precisely the ground of her most urgent questions. This book is based on these questions, for I see her central subject as the role of manners and society in human affairs. Essentially, I am trying to do three things here: to assess Edith Wharton's qualities and contributions as a novelist, to explore ways of analyzing the novel of manners and the meaning of society in fiction, and to provide careful and broad-based readings of her three most important novels, *The House of Mirth, The Custom of the Country,* and *The Age of Innocence.* Each aim suggests a different strategy: the first, a comprehensive examination of all of Wharton's fiction; the second, a broader theoretical and technical study of novels of manners and the traditions they form; the third, a series of extended explications of one text at a time. But before one can discuss the traditions and range of the novel of manners, one must find ways of talking about particular novels of manners. And before one can describe a novelist's qualities, one must have an accurate account of what is going on in her particular fictions. My bias, then, is toward careful analysis of the immediate text and deliberately tentative approaches to the problem of how to read novels of manners, and this bias is reflected in both the strategy and the limitations of this book. Although Edith Wharton began writing novels of manners with *The Valley of Decision* (1902) and was still writing one, *The Buccaneers,* when she died in 1937, and although most of her intervening works are novels of manners, I deal extensively with only three. Some of her other good novels—*Ethan Frome, The Reef,* and *Summer*—diverge slightly from the emphasis of the novel of manners, and some of her later novels of manners, such as *Glimpses of the Moon* and *Twilight Sleep*, are simply not good books. But my main reason for spending time with *The House of Mirth, The Custom of the Country,* and *The Age of Innocence* is that they are clearly her best work, her most illuminating studies of manners, and a distinguished contribution to American literature, a contribution demanding more painstaking examination than it has had to date. In my general comments on Wharton's themes and procedures, however, I refer to her fiction as a whole.

Because I am interested both in establishing ways of reading novels of manners and in providing analyses of three novels, I have organized the book by approaches to fiction, each explored theoretically and then exemplified in the particular insights it affords in the three novels. The six chapters could be seen as representing six familiar bases of novelistic analysis—theme, plot, setting, characterization, style, and scene—but I have varied each approach to fit the special emphasis on manners and to give new power and range to the concept of society in fiction. The first chapter is the broadest and most theoretical, describing Wharton's general assumptions about the relation of the individual to society and setting off these assumptions against a nineteenth-century context, both American and European. Rather than define a formal tradition, however, I emphasize in this preliminary chapter the specialness of Edith Wharton's basic beliefs about manners and the individual.

The remaining chapters deal with those knottier ideas peculiar to narrative, the ones that are never stated but appear implicitly in the kinds of stories told and the methods of telling them. It is in these chapters that I am working out ways of describing society in fiction. Chapter 2 deals with the stories Wharton tells, their dynamics, their crises, their underlying expectations. On the one hand, I assess here the dynamic elements of society revealed in the workings and powers of the plots themselves; on the other, I describe a buried fable in Wharton's fiction, a private story involving the release of the individual from class-dominated ways of seeing. Chapter 3 veers the most from traditional modes of novelistic analysis, for it is not so much concerned with setting as with the social setting, with those patterns of detail and gesture that constitute the manners of a social order. My assumption here is that the basic nature of a society consists of the sum of its manners and their supporting assumptions and that the novelist reveals this nature by the immediate depiction of manners. Through close analysis of the way Wharton presents manners in her novels, I describe her implicit assessments of the social orders themselves. The fourth chapter measures the most intimate power of a social order, the shaping of the individual soul. I am concerned with two aspects of characterization in the novel of manners, the creation of secondary characters who represent segments of the social order and the development of substantial figures through whom the psychological impact of society can be estimated. In analyzing Wharton's prose style in chapter 5, I focus on the ways in which her diction and syntax create subtle anticipations in our reading, reflecting the power of a social order to enmesh itself in the very medium through which one tries to describe it.

Like chapter 3, the final chapter adapts a traditional approach to fiction to the special substance of the novel of manners, here focusing on a particular kind of scene, the formal social gathering. These scenes are clearly of great importance to the novelist of manners, but the range of emphasis possible within them is wide indeed, and Wharton's handling of such scenes brings into focus all her special qualities as a novelist. In such circumstances, with conventions so elevated as to define a ritual, with characters acting under maximum constraint and surveillance, she shows manners at their most influential as individuals make their most desperate expressions of self. It is in the context of my analysis of these scenes that I also summarize Edith Wharton's overall limitations and achievements.

The Individual in Society
Character and Personage

EDITH WHARTON'S MAJOR subject is the impact of social organization, an issue closely allied with the thematic base of the novel of manners. Her most important assumptions about human experience can thus be usefully examined through the question, What is the relation of the individual to society? In this chapter I define these attitudes in general ways, providing a framework for the more specific analyses to follow. Except in the broadest sense I am not trying to place Wharton in a tradition. The important literary influences on her fiction come from quite varied sources, from writers as diverse as Balzac and Flaubert, George Eliot and James, and she absorbs quite different things from each writer. If she does not obviously fit into a particular formal tradition, however, there is a broader thematic context within which her attitudes and their implications assume their proper significance. In the early part of the chapter I describe those nineteenth-century methods of emphasizing individuality that clarify Wharton's general orientation. Then I turn to some special developments in American literature, peculiar images of society and of the self, that locate more exactly the nature and importance of Edith Wharton's beliefs.

Aspiration and the Individual

The novel of manners shows the relation of individual and social convention to be more serious and more difficult than the characters had expected. It depends upon a sufficient community of values that crises in the personal life can be related to public events, to marriage or divorce, social rise or fall, shifts in money or power, communal judgments. Yet at its most characteristic the novel of manners assumes a deeply problematic relation between self and society. It is for this reason that the novel of manners flourishes in and against a context of romanticism. As long as the individual is regarded as a distinct combination of basically shareable traits, he can be characterized in generic terms. Although he may deliberately conceal part of himself, his nature will be essentially comprehensible in the public arena; he can be defined by reference to moral universals and to a social order, nothing in him being ultimately inaccessible to public understanding. It is this attitude that informs the world of *Tom Jones*, for example. On the other hand, when the individual is seen as a bundle of emotional and psychological complexities and when, in addition, he is valued precisely for his unique feelings, his nature remains opaque to the public eye. Whatever in him can be defined in social terms is likely to be misleading or compromised.

This attitude toward the individual is exactly what began to emerge in the sentimental tradition of the later eighteenth century and developed as a central feature of romanticism. One of the broadest thematic tendencies in nineteenth-century fiction is to pit an idealistic, yearning individual against a stifling or mean-spirited social order. For all their differences, such figures as Julien Sorel, Eugène de Rastignac, Emma Bovary, Hester Prynne, Captain Ahab, Huck Finn, Dorothea Brooke, and Isabel Archer assume much of their dynamism within this configuration. What allows the struggle to be forceful is the possibility of separating between social and nonsocial definitions of the self. The romantic fervor to reveal and to sympathize with the hidden needs of the self clarified for the novel of manners the other side of a polarity, not only between self and society but also between private and public selves. But to disclose the private self so as to make it an attractive and worthy antagonist of society involves serious difficulties, and some of the major nineteenth-century approaches to the self can help us understand Edith Wharton's procedures and her problems.

The most compelling means of articulating private feelings was to show them clustered about certain ideals or aspirations. From some model other than the immediate social order—from literature or religion, a glorified past or a different social class—the individual may derive patterns of conduct and desire not only alien to, but better than, those of his own class, and the conflict between self and society becomes more powerful for its clear basis in a conflict of classes or ideals. One of the common forms of this antagonism is what Émile Durkheim described as a conflict between culturally inspired goals and socially prescribed ways of attaining them. Julien Sorel's feelings, for example, cluster around aspirations determined by the earlier heroic era of Napoleon, but he initially moves in a bourgeois society devoted to mundane methods of personal advancement. Similarly, Dorothea Brooke's ardent longings take their shape from a deeply religious past personified in the figure of Saint Theresa, and she can find no adequate field for service in the provincial society of Middlemarch.

It is this form of the conflict that motivates Edith Wharton's firmest presentation of individual idealism, *The Valley of Decision*. Set in eighteenth-century Italy, this historical novel tells the story of young Odo Valsecca, a boy of noble birth who, after a varied education and an exposure to the violent contrasts in the lives of his countrymen, becomes Duke of Pianura and tries, on the whole unsuccessfully, to bring about greater liberty and better living conditions for his people. In his youth Odo imbibes his aspirations from the frescoes on the walls of a deserted family chapel. The face of Saint Francis teaches him to love the poor; the picture of Saint George, reinforced by tales of his own family's martial adventures, fosters a desire for heroic service. During his apprenticeship to the trivial conventions of aristocratic life, Odo seems to forget his ideals, but his reading of Rousseau and his friendship with scientific freethinkers and advocates of liberty reaffirm and give focus to his earlier aspirations. Because she clearly defines the intellectual and physical tyranny of the church and nobility, Wharton can direct Odo's libertarian zeal at specific abuses, generating in her fiction the excitement of "that vast noiseless labor of the spirit going on everywhere beneath the social surface."[1]

Once in office, however, Odo learns that the noblest aims may not survive intact when applied to the actual situation, and his struggle with his society begins in earnest. However badly oppressed the peasants have been, they resist Odo's attempts to alleviate their condition when reform cuts into the privileges of the clergy and the nobility. Habitual reverence proves a conservative force. More immediately, Odo discovers that he must constantly repurchase his own power by complicity and intrigue with the various nobles of his court. And even within himself Odo finds pressures to com-

[1] *The Valley of Decision* (New York, 1902), II, 94.

promise his aspirations as he comes under the spell of the aesthetic splendor surrounding him: "He had known moments of happiness . . . when his opportunities had seemed as boundless as his dreams, and he had not yet learned that the sovereign's power may be a kind of spiritual prison to the man. Since then, indeed, he had known another kind of happiness . . . but this was when he had realized that he lived in a prison, and had begun to admire the sumptuous adornment of its walls."[2]

Although Odo Valsecca is a weaker and less interesting character than Julien Sorel or Dorothea Brooke, his plight, like theirs, can move us because the aspirations that define his conflict with society are coherent and, in their context, attractive. Not all individuals, however, are idealists, and even yearning protagonists may have their desires shaped in far less coherent ways than Odo Valsecca. Then it becomes more difficult to disclose those feelings that isolate the protagonist and create a moving struggle with society. Flaubert explores the problem at length in *Madame Bovary,* where the yearning self confusedly searches for models and ideals by which it can justify its own sense of superiority to its dull surroundings. For Emma Bovary is not, like Don Quixote, primarily misled by her readings or by romantic conventions. There is some intuitive core of her which desperately seeks expression and fulfillment through whatever conventions may be at hand. Although, like Dorothea Brooke, she draws early inspirations from a religious past, her education in the convent does not make her desire self-sacrifice or service. Rather it awakens, through her senses, a mystical languor that responds less to dogma than to the sexual undertones of religious metaphors. Her exposure to historical romances, keepsake albums, and eighteenth-century love songs, in turn, associates her newly discovered sentiments with picturesque scenes and the life of the court. Thus by the time of her first encounter with aristocratic life at the Vaubyessard ball, Emma is ready to transfer her feelings from a sentimentalized past to the upper classes. Her successive disillusionments are not really educative, for the inner yearning survives its discarded forms. Emma remains certain of only one thing—that she does not belong in, and cannot be measured by, the one reality she knows, social life in

[2] *Valley,* II, 179.

Yonville. And her aspirations, erratic and vague as they are, assure her of her superiority.

Were we actually to meet an Emma Bovary, we would scorn her ill-founded pretensions, and this is the socially based habit that the novelist must offset in dramatizing the struggle of the individual with society. Flaubert's success here is chiefly due to his inventive use of detail. He evokes Emma's feelings with clarity and power by allowing them to play indirectly against her sensory perception. While her longings and illusions transfigure the distant landscape and the symbolic reminders of another life, her impatience with reality as she knows it emphasizes in monotonous precision all the objects, sounds, and smells that surround her daily life. In such ways Flaubert shows us that even Emma's own words are inadequate to the nature of her yearnings.

But Flaubert is also appealing to a broader inheritance from romanticism. By separating the tawdriness of Emma's purposes from the purity of her desire, he indicates that characteristic shift of focus in which the outward goal becomes less important than the subjective experience of yearning, as in the Faustian affirmation of endless striving as itself the grandest individual posture. Even without clear and coherent models, aspiration for its own sake may legitimize an individual identity that is quite independent of its social surroundings. The resulting widespread phenomenon is described in Walter Houghton's *The Victorian Frame of Mind* as "aspiration without an object."[3] Although ideal aspirations were highly valued in the romantic and Victorian ages, the objectives themselves were losing credibility. And aspiration, in Houghton's words, became "an exciting experience instead of an inspiring one." Figures like Browning's Rabbi Ben Ezra were more likely to have their eyes on themselves in the act of aspiring than on any well-defined goals.

This looser and more aimless aspiration is the distinguishing feature of most of Edith Wharton's major characters. Cut off from faith in absolute goals or in noble models from the past, they retain idealistic passions chiefly in the form of emotional excitement. And since they find themselves placed near the peak of a limited social structure, they cannot participate in that ascendancy

---

[3]Walter Houghton, *The Victorian Frame of Mind* (New Haven, 1964), pp. 291-97.

through the classes which further defines the individuality and aspiration of characters like Julien Sorel and Eugène de Rastignac. But Wharton does not seem to be satisfied with vague aspiration. She formulates idealistic passions in collapsible metaphoric phrases or in romantic clichés, as if she distrusted her characters' feelings. Although she sympathizes with their finer instincts, she cannot create for her readers a firm belief in the capacities of the human spirit to define and pursue a significant object of aspiration. Too often her protagonists' feelings, however delicate and sympathetic, gather about ideals subtly shaped by their immediate societies; unlike Emma Bovary, whose aspirations at least arise from something outside her direct communal experience, they bind themselves by desire as well as habit to what they see about them. And when their reading seems to create an independent critical perspective, as is the case with many of Wharton's young men, they can establish neither definite nor influential relations, even of antagonism, between their poetic theories and their actual behavior.

There is, then, a potential failure in the confrontation of self and society in Edith Wharton's fiction. Unlike her major nineteenth-century predecessors in the novel of manners, she does not believe that subjective yearnings are as legitimate a focus of interest as objective patterns of behavior. She is consistently more effective at defining the social aspects of the self than the personal. She is unable or unwilling to endow her characters with the desperate longing of an Emma Bovary, the ardor of a Dorothea Brooke, or the eager inward freedom of an Isabel Archer. This is more than a matter of taking sides, of preferring social coherence and mutual regard to the excesses of romantic individualism, a posture Wharton generally shares with such writers as Austen, Cooper, George Eliot, and Howells. It is a matter of expression, dramatization, belief, not of moral judgment. Even when the spiritual yearnings of her characters are attractive, she dooms them in their very presentation. The precision and extent of her social analysis, in contrast, reveal an orientation away from the possibilities of individual fulfillment and toward everything that limits it.

An American Image of Society

Although romantic individualism helps to locate what is problematic in the self's ties to society, it does not determine the characteristic thrust of the novel of manners, a mode committed as well to the inescapable reality of social experience. Thus while the novelist of manners tries to generate sympathy for the finer yearnings of his characters, he also carefully observes the social forms that constrain them. The contrast between open vistas and enclosed corridors, for example, haunts readers of both *Middlemarch* and *The Portrait of a Lady,* strengthening their concern for Dorothea and Isabel. Part of the characterization in a novel of manners, then, involves the careful differentiation of social and personal aspects of the self, and this art requires exacting definition of the social context. As the background is determined more precisely, the individual emerges more distinctly against it. The exactness of the social context depends, in turn, on the novelist's differentiation within it. That is why class division provides such advantages for characterization in the novel of manners. As Lionel Trilling observes, the realization of social class enables us to see people more precisely in their difference, their specialness, their solidity.[4] Similarly, a class-structured view of reality allows the novelist to delineate substantially the restrictive qualities of a character's immediate society. Thus we can sympathize with Emma Bovary, not only because of Flaubert's sensory revelation of her yearnings, but also because an existing class structure allows him to plot with deadly precision the confinement of life at Yonville. Even though Emma idealizes aristocratic life at the Vaubyessard ball and sentimentally transfigures the country gentleman, Rodolphe Boulanger, the observable contrast between aristocratic and bourgeois manners makes Charles Bovary and Homais, the pharmacist, all the more repugnant to her. When Rodolphe deserts her and betrays her hopes, he sends his note in a basket of apricots. He can perform even a cruel act with a delicate gesture. But when Emma sees her husband eating the apricots and spitting the pits into his hand, the reality to which she is consigned focuses all her scattered torment so precisely that her nerves collapse.

[4]"Art and Fortune," in *The Liberal Imagination,* esp. pp. 261-62.

This entire dialogue between social and personal aspects of the self, however, undergoes important shifts in American fiction, shifts in regard to both the social image and the sense of what constitutes the self. It is against the context of these American tendencies that one can recognize most clearly the significance of Edith Wharton's beliefs. One source for shifts in the American image of society was the widespread assumption that the new democratic society was relatively undifferentiated, so that the American, as Tocqueville puts it, "sees around him on every hand men differing but little from one another; he cannot turn his mind to any one portion of mankind without expanding and dilating his thought till it embraces the whole."[5] This assumption has become the basis for the familiar argument that American society has been deficient in materials for the novel of manners and that American fiction has consequently turned to abstract, symbolic, or ideological matters, to the methods of the romance.[6]

Although this argument underestimates the extent to which American writers have succeeded with the novel of manners, it still has value for reminding us of some obvious differences between nineteenth-century fiction in America and in Europe. For if Cooper and Howells, for example, do in fact present distinctions in social

[5]Alexis de Tocqueville, *Democracy in America*, ed. Phillips Bradley (New York, 1945), II, 16.

[6]The stock sources for this argument are Cooper's and James's famous lists (in *Notions of the Americans* and *Hawthorne*) of America's deficiencies for the novelist of manners. Lionel Trilling observes in *The Liberal Imagination* ("Manners, Morals, and the Novel" and "Art and Fortune") that the real basis of the novel—a tension between classes, throwing manners into observable relief—has never existed here. Richard Chase, *The American Novel and Its Tradition* (Garden City, N. Y., 1957) sees American fiction, as a result, turning from manners and social portraiture to the psychological possibilities of the romance. Marius Bewley, *The Eccentric Design: Form in the Classic American Novel* (New York, 1963), points up the difficulties of analyzing reality through social observation when existing social conditions provide few substantialities. He finds the basis for form in American literature in a more abstract reality created through personal tensions or through conflicts of more or less disembodied ideas, like aristocracy and democracy or wilderness and industrial civilization. And Richard Poirier, *A World Elsewhere* (New York, 1966), shows how several American writers turn away from social and economic conventions that trammel their finer instincts, trying instead to build in words an environment more congenial to a free consciousness. For an argument that this general reading of American fiction is deficient, see James W. Tuttleton, *The Novel of Manners in America* (Chapel Hill, 1972), especially chapter 1.

class and exact observations of manners as parts of their characterization and if their social worlds are more complex than those
of Hawthorne and Melville, these same social worlds are still quite
thin compared to those, say, of Balzac. The relative lack of differentiation in the social world is one of the major elements of the
varied image of society in American fiction. At its extreme this
image posits a special configuration of individual against society—
the self against the mass—as when Hester Prynne mounts the
scaffold before a thousand eyes. For all her differences from her
American predecessors, Edith Wharton inherits this configuration
of self against mass, adapting it imaginatively as the basis for her
formal scenes, as I will illustrate in the concluding chapter.

Even more revealing than the extent to which social distinctions
are observed in American fiction is the manner in which such
distinctions are presented. James Fenimore Cooper illustrates one
important tendency in American fiction by his efforts to subordinate social observation to matters of principle. In his fiction
as well as his polemical writings, he is repeatedly concerned with
the possibilities of a good civilization in the new country and with
the threats to it. He observes in his preface to *Satanstoe* that a
chronicle of manners takes on its true value "when customs are
connected to principles, in their origin, development, or end."
What this reduces to in practice is his habit of creating models of
conduct. It is not simply that Corny Littlepage has different manners from Jason Newcome, the New Englander, or Guert Ten
Eyck, the Dutch Albanian, or Bulstrode, the British officer, but
that Corny's manners are exemplary for the growth of American
civilization and that Jason's, in particular, represent some of the
worst dangers to it. Cooper believes strongly in the power of
manners to influence the whole of character and feeling. Even in
his digressions from the drawing room to the perils of the woods
he shows the quality of personal response to be deeply affected
by training, habits, models, and social background, so that the
wilderness often serves as the ultimate test of certain manners and
the character they build. But this is to say there are good manners
and bad manners, not simply differences of class or background.
The novelist's social differentiation becomes a moral art. In *The
Pioneers,* one of Cooper's best novels and very much a novel of
manners, most of the class distinctions belong to the comic realm

of minor figures—Remarkable Pettibone, the New England servant who won't serve; Ben Pump, the British steward; M. le Quoi, the French storekeeper. But the serious class conflict emerges between Judge Temple, on the one hand, and Richard Jones and Hiram Doolittle, on the other. It is a conflict that Cooper sees as involving right and wrong ways to build the new community. Thus the major differentiation of manners rests less on the assumed complexity of society itself than on the conflict of principles at the core of the book. What this implies is that the variegation of the social scene is not the given basis on which we understand the complexity of character and class background but rather the evidence of contradiction in the moral direction of the country.

William Dean Howells, too, concerns himself with the possibilities of civilization in America, especially in a relatively late book like *A Hazard of New Fortunes,* in which he shows that the melting pot does not work, that differences in social background prevent the expression of human decency. But Howells is more characteristically interested in the common life of humanity, and this interest leads him, too, into a specialized version of social differentiation. He is a careful observer of social distinction, and his novels of manners abound with substantial detail. But this detail has as often the function of humanizing as of socially locating his characters. Repeatedly he stresses common problems, recognizable feelings, using such phrases as "the loud obstinacy of a man whose women always have their way" to refer the character to the generality of human nature. And his characteristic emphasis on the intimate, daily wear of human life is more a matter of moral energy, personal resiliency, and family dynamics than of the personal background of manners. Thus there is a critical difference between the fundamental humanity and the specialized social conduct of his characters, and this difference is one of his major subjects as a novelist of manners. He does not accept easily the importance of social distinction, as is clear in his central statement of judgment in *The Rise of Silas Lapham:* "it is certain that our manners and customs go for more in life than our qualities. The price that we pay for civilization is the fine yet impassable differentiation of these."[7] Thus while Howells delineates social distinction

---

[7]William D. Howells, *The Rise of Silas Lapham* (Boston, 1885), p. 509.

clearly and portrays manners in detail, there is a counterpressure in his novels toward the common substance of humanity. Social differentiation appears as a superimposition, genuine enough but perhaps accidental and certainly pernicious; it belies the most important parts of the characters.

The examples of Cooper and Howells suggest that for American novelists the very presentation of social distinction is a slightly ominous proceeding, an acknowledgment of social conditions that make them uneasy. Many American novelists, including Cooper and Howells, tend to locate outward distinctions more by juxtaposing sections of the country or by bringing together Americans and Europeans than by delineating class divisions within one locale. Thus the characters often discover differences of person relatively late, by travel or occupation or by the intrusion of outsiders, and the distinctions come as a shock. This shock—the feeling of Silas Lapham before Bromfield Corey or of Corny Littlepage first making the acquaintance of Jason Newcome—is the characterological projection of the novelist's own uneasiness. It might even develop into a major fictional issue, a questioning of the character's conception of reality or a test of his integrity, especially when the contrast in manners is international. One thinks in this regard of Redburn landing at Liverpool, of Hawthorne's Hilda walking into Saint Peter's in Rome, of Christopher Newman entering the Bellegarde mansion, and, more imaginatively, of the Connecticut Yankee, Hank Morgan, waking up in Camelot.

There is another kind of uneasiness that is common to American novels of manners, an uneasiness not so much with the fact of distinction in society as with the subtle basis of it, manners themselves. A wide range of characters in American fiction approach social experience with a disquieting seriousness, a distrust of assumption. They demand open, clear statements of the rules of behavior and regard with suspicion, impatience, or moral indifference those manners that refuse to be stated but are absorbed and taken for granted within a social group. Whatever cannot be directly explained or simply imitated emerges as unimportant or threatening or, more likely, both. Of course, one reason American characters can rarely act on assumed codes is that the codes are often unknown. When Silas Lapham's family desperately consult an etiquette book to find out how to dress and behave at a dinner

party among Boston's socially elite, they typify and explain the
seriousness of the American character confronting social assumptions. Like Cooper's Jason Newcome, Adams's Senator Ratcliffe,
Christopher Newman, Jay Gatsby, and Thomas Sutpen, they act
on strangely contradictory beliefs—that they can "get" the right
manners if they set their minds to it, that manners are a foolish
acquirement, and that they are vaguely dangerous. James acutely
probes this seriousness and uneasiness in *The Europeans*. Here he
shows his Americans operating under loose and uncertain codes of
social behavior while being rigidly bound to an abstract conception
of duty. His European baroness, in contrast, cares little about
abstract obligations, but she acts on an elaborate set of habits in
the actual contingencies of social intercourse. In simplified form,
the contrast is between morals without manners and manners
without morals. Although Mr. Wentworth regards the visit of his
European cousins as a test of his family and his friends, a test to
be conducted with high moral seriousness, he cannot locate the
specific ground of the test, cannot attach his moral sense clearly
to the immediate issues of behavior. When Mme. Münster takes his
arm to be escorted into the house, he does not know whether he
offered his arm, whether he should have offered it if he did not,
or whether the baroness should have taken an unoffered arm. A
seemingly unimportant gesture provokes moral uncertainty, and
Wentworth can feel only a vague suspicion.

   In contrast to the European novel of manners, which may show
society to be problematic but still takes the influence of manners
for granted, the American novel of manners often makes the
domain of manners a source of uneasiness. Insofar as principles of
conduct are being encouraged in the fiction, distinctions in manners become evidence not of social diversity but of moral
antagonism. And if the differentiation of social context allows the
European novelist to individualize the personal qualities of his
characters, the differentiation revealed by a writer like Howells
serves rather to set off the common humanity of the protagonist.
The novelist's uneasiness with social contrasts and the characters'
suspicions of assumed and complex codes of behavior both point
to the same phenomenon characteristic of the American novel of
manners: society is something "out there," alien, perhaps beguiling
but also dangerous. Central characters in American fiction are

seldom presented as "in" society, at least in the sense that Eugène de Rastignac, Emma Bovary, and Dorothea Brooke are in society. Instead of appearing enclosed in the constrictions of manners, class, social history, and shared assumptions about behavior, the American character more typically begins his adventure outside of society.[8] If social entanglement figures in European fiction as a prison from which the individual may emerge, it assumes the guise in American fiction of a potential trap. The reality of the individual's ties to society is not given or assumed as part of the characterization; it appears rather as an event, a test, something to which the character will be exposed.

Character and Personage

Thus far I have been stressing the social image in American novels of manners. Even more important in suggesting the specialness of American fiction is the image of the self. In contrast to the European novelist of manners, who carefully differentiates personal from social aspects of the self, American writers tend to give primacy, both in time and importance, to an unconditioned self. Cooper is obviously an exception to this principle, but even he provides an early basis for it in Leatherstocking's famous distinction between "gifts" and "natur'," a doctrine which acknowledges the importance in immediate behavior of social circumstances (gifts) but which also suggests that "the man" (nature) transcends "the conduct." And Howells's lament at the contrast between "manners" and "qualities" is another assertion of belief in a self who does not need to be defined against a social network but whose personal nature is independent and directly knowable. Pushed to an extreme, this American self seems even to have a choice whether to enter into social entanglements at all, as in this attractive and audacious statement: " 'Know all men by these presents, that I,

---

[8]This observation, of course, is not original; it has appeared in many contexts and is developed in detail in R. W. B. Lewis, *The American Adam: Innocence, Tragedy, and Tradition in the Nineteenth Century* (Chicago, 1955).

Henry Thoreau, do not wish to be regarded as a member of any incorporated society which I have not joined.' "[9]

The significance of this unconditioned self becomes especially apparent in the fiction of Henry James and F. Scott Fitzgerald, but the basic theories appear in the writings of Ralph Waldo Emerson, especially in the essay "Self-Reliance."

I ask primary evidence that you are a man, and refuse this appeal from the man to his actions. I know that for myself it makes no difference whether I do or forbear those actions which are reckoned excellent. I cannot consent to pay for a privilege where I have intrinsic right. Few and mean as my gifts may be, I actually am, and do not need for my own assurance or the assurance of my fellows any secondary testimony. . . .

The objection to conforming to usages that have become dead to you is that it scatters your force. It loses your time and blurs the impression of your character. If you maintain a dead church, contribute to a dead Bible-society, vote with a great party either for the government or against it, spread your table like base house-keepers,—under all these screens I have difficulty to detect the precise man you are: and of course so much force is withdrawn from your proper life.[10]

It is the person who discovers himself enmeshed in social circumstances that must "pay" for the privilege of being an individual; Emerson's "man," on the contrary, has "intrinsic right" simply to *be*. In his characteristic preference for *being* rather than *doing,* a preference shared by Thoreau and Henry James, Emerson dismisses socially perceptible gestures as "screens" to one's "proper life." Of course "the precise man" in this passage is far from precise; since it is only the "secondary testimony" that Emerson can specify, the proper individual must emerge largely through negative definition. As he says in another context: "The spirit is not helpless or needful of mediate organs. It has plentiful powers and direct effects. I am explained without explaining, I am felt without acting, and where I am not."[11] But by distinguishing primary from secondary evidence, immediate from mediate relations, and direct from indirect effects, Emerson does indicate in a more positive

[9] "Civil Disobedience," in *Walden and Other Writings,* ed. Brooks Atkinson (New York, 1937), p. 649.

[10] *Emerson's Complete Works,* Riverside Ed. (Boston, 1883), II, 54-55.

[11] Emerson, III, 75.

way the working power of his key term *character*. Although character is not evidenced by actions in the ordinary sense, it has "force" and can impress itself upon others directly and immediately. This force can be scattered or withdrawn by social activity, a reminder that the vital primary self predates and transcends social experience entirely. Character is allied to spirit; it resides in the soul and is preeminently moral. For Emerson character is an article of faith, an assumption; he can assert that it is the core of the proper individual, but to show its operations or define its qualities further would be to use "mediate organs" and circumstantial indirection.

This Emersonian faith in character did not need the metaphysical support of American transcendentalism, and it had followers of a less theoretical cast far outside the circle of Emerson's own associates. It is the quality in Emerson that most attracted Henry James: "The genius itself it seems to me impossible to contest—I mean the genius for seeing character as a real and supreme thing. . . . No one has had so steady and constant, and above all so natural, a vision of what we require and what we are capable of in the way of aspiration and independence. With Emerson it is ever the special capacity for moral experience—always that and only that."[12]

But James had another side, the side that looked in the novel for "the air of reality (solidity of specification)" and said, "We know a man imperfectly until we know his society, and we but half know a society until we know its manners."[13] It was this other side that allowed James to see so clearly the fictional possibilities of Emerson's concept of character by comparison with its alternative, *personage*. He uses the terms to analyze Isabel Archer's relationship to Lord Warburton, as Warburton is about to propose to her:

She had received a strong impression of his being a "personage," and she had occupied herself in examining the image so conveyed. At the risk of adding to the evidence of her self-sufficiency it must be said that there had been moments when this possibility of admiration by a personage represented to her an aggression almost to the degree of an affront, quite to the degree of an inconvenience. She had never yet known a personage; there had been no

---

[12]"Emerson," in *Partial Portraits* (New York, 1888), pp. 8-9.

[13]Ibid., p. 3.

personages, in this sense, in her life; there were probably none such at all in her native land. When she had thought of individual eminence she had thought of it on the basis of character and wit—of what one might like in a gentleman's mind and in his talk. She herself was a character—she couldn't help being aware of that; and hitherto her visions of a completed consciousness had concerned themselves largely with moral images—things as to which the question would be whether they pleased her sublime soul. Lord Warburton loomed up before her, largely and brightly, as a collection of attributes and powers which were not to be measured by this simple rule, but which demanded a different sort of appreciation—an appreciation that the girl, with her habit of judging quickly and freely, felt she lacked patience to bestow. He appeared to demand of her something that no one else, as it were, had presumed to do. What she felt was that a territorial, a political, a social magnate had conceived the design of drawing her into the system in which he rather invidiously lived and moved. A certain instinct, not imperious, but persuasive, told her to resist— murmured to her that virtually she had a system and an orbit of her own. . . . Furthermore there was a young man lately come from America who had no system at all, but who had a character of which it was useless for her to try to persuade herself that the impression on her mind had been light.[14]

For Isabel a personage is defined by what Emerson calls secondary testimony—his attributes and powers, his social and political connections. The threat of a personage cannot be distinguished from the threat of the system in which he moves. In regard to the system, of course, what Isabel most fears is entrapment, but the nature of the entrapment emerges more clearly in her feelings about Warburton personally. Whereas in normal usage an affront is a worse offense than an inconvenience, and an aggression worse than either, James elaborately inverts the terms to show exactly what kind of aggression Warburton represents. He is not an active physical or sexual assailant; this role is reserved for Caspar Goodwood, who is preeminently a character. Instead, Warburton demands of Isabel a complex and detailed effort simply to be appreciated as a human being. That is, to have a personal relationship with Warburton, Isabel must involve herself with his society and its manners and assumptions. The patient observation required of her is an inconvenience of a grave sort, an expenditure of her own energy on a social system. Thus the entrapment Isabel fears

---

[14]*The Portrait of a Lady* (New York, 1908), I, 143-44. Without attempting here to enumerate the relative merits of the first edition (1881) and the New York revision, I have used the text of the latter because, in the passages cited, it defines more clearly the issues I am examining.

is less a constriction than a dissipation of her "sublime soul" in a complex of particularities, a scattering of her force. What she stands to lose is her own system and orbit, that is, her integrity.

A character presents no such threat. He is apprehended immediately without the implication of a social system or of detailed observation. Instead of demanding perception and patient understanding, he makes an impression, as Emerson said he would, and this impression can be judged directly and simply by its correspondence with one's own soul. For Isabel, then, the difference between personage and character is as much a matter of how one perceives and judges people as it is an objective distinction. Like so many figures in American fiction, she believes it both possible and desirable to know men and women individually without having to account for their behavior or their society. Her habit of judging quickly and freely shows a mind so attuned to dealing with characters that when she confronts a personage she can only grapple with the "strong impression" of his being one.

Apart from Isabel's distinctions, however, the passage raises important issues about characterization. As Isabel must engage much of her energy in perceiving and relating herself to a personage, the novelist presenting such a figure must expend himself in observing and delineating his behavior and the social network within which it has significance. Again like Isabel, the novelist dealing with a character can be more sweeping and immediate; he can use the kind of shorthand that James here refers to as "moral images." The passage itself is one example of this procedure; it analyzes Warburton's nature and especially his relationship to Isabel on a highly abstract plane, disregarding the particular forms of his behavior. The moral image can also take such a form as the following exchange between Ralph Touchett and Isabel about Henrietta Stackpole: " 'She's too personal—considering that she expects other people not to be. She walks in without knocking at the door.' 'Yes,' Isabel admitted, 'she doesn't sufficiently recognise the existence of knockers; and indeed I'm not sure that she doesn't think them rather a pretentious ornament. She thinks one's door should stand ajar.' "[15] Here Henrietta's character emerges

---

[15]Ibid., I, 129.

directly; her manners, only indirectly, through the image of walking in without knocking.

But the exchange illustrates another implication of the moral image. Our attention is drawn less to Henrietta's nature than to the nature of her relationships with other individuals. In fact, if a character is apprehended immediately through the impression made on someone else, he emerges primarily as in a certain relationship, and it is the relationship itself that the moral image defines, without the mediation of observable manners. On the other hand, the fictional procedure for developing a personage—delineation of his behavior, dress, position, surroundings—defines his nature against the set of manners and assumptions that make up his society. His relationship to another individual will either take its shape within the framework of this society or, if the other individual comes from a different social order, it will have to be transmitted through conflicting social assumptions. The distinction between character and personage, then, involves the conception of what a human being is, how he is connected with society, and how he can relate to other persons.

The distinction also suggests alternate ways in which novelists can approach their fictional beings. In this sense, many major American novelists seize on characters rather than on personages. This is obviously true of those who can be considered romancers, but it also pertains to those, like James and Fitzgerald, who seem to be writing novels of manners. To clarify the meaning and the attractiveness of this orientation toward character, one can usefully look further into the example of James, who by his sound recognition of the claims of society seems to differ markedly from such writers as Hawthorne and Melville. And to make the case extreme, let me illustraté his approach to one of his most conspicuous personages—Madame Merle—in her most celebrated argument with Isabel Archer, an exchange that seems, at first glance, to belong purely to the novel of manners:

"When you've lived as long as I you'll see that every human being has his shell and that you must take the shell into account. By the shell I mean the whole envelope of circumstances. There's no such thing as an isolated man or woman; we're each of us made up of some cluster of appurtenances. What shall we call our 'self'? Where does it begin? where does it end? It overflows into everything that belongs to us—and then it flows back again. I know a large part of myself is in the clothes I choose to wear. I've a great respect for *things*! One's self—for other people—is one's expression of one's self; and one's house, one's furniture, one's garments, the books one reads, the company one keeps—these things are all expressive."

. . . "I don't agree with you. I think just the other way. I don't know whether I succeed in expressing myself, but I know that nothing else expresses me. Nothing that belongs to me is any measure of me; everything's on the contrary a limit, a barrier, and a perfectly arbitrary one. Certainly the clothes which, as you say, I choose to wear, don't express me; and heaven forbid they should!"

"You dress very well," Madame Merle lightly interposed.

"Possibly; but I don't care to be judged by that. My clothes may express the dressmaker, but they don't express me. To begin with it's not my own choice that I wear them; they're imposed upon me by society."

"Should you prefer to go without them?" Madame Merle enquired in a tone which virtually terminated the discussion.[16]

In both manner and matter James makes here one of his most elegant cases for seeing human beings as personages, as existing in an almost infinite web of connectedness. Some forty years later Edith Wharton will argue, in *The Writing of Fiction*, that individuals must be recognized as the products of particular material and social circumstances, that the personality flows imperceptibly into adjacent people and things. Since Madame Merle so clearly anticipates Wharton's theoretical position, and her narrative practice as well, it is pertinent to see what James does with his personage. One is tempted to regard her here as speaking for the author, especially as Isabel's education in the novel will bring her closer to Madame Merle's position. Furthermore, she clearly has the advantage in argumentative skill, for Isabel is too deeply involved with her own feelings to comprehend or control her opponent. Madame Merle's deft verbal manners muster the full resources of the personage as a socially connected creature; they illustrate in practice what she says in theory, and they show in passing how good James was at the methods of the novel of manners.

The confrontation of Isabel and Madame Merle is reminiscent of the conversations between Julien Sorel and Madame de Rênal, or between Eugène de Rastignac and the Viscountess de Beauséant; that is, it echoes the traditional scenes in novels of manners when

[16]Ibid., I, 287-88.

the aspiring young man from the provinces confronts an adept representative of the urban haute bourgeoisie or aristocracy. Against a set of manners he does not recognize and class assumptions he does not share, both controlled habitually and with grace, the novitiate must depend only on ingenuousness and charm. But there is an important difference. The confrontation between Isabel and Madame Merle is not a meeting and jarring of two social classes. Isabel may be from the provinces of upstate New York, but she is not conceived or presented as from any particular class. And what class, or even nationality, does Madame Merle represent? She is simply and magnificently *in society;* Isabel is simply and charmingly outside. In other words, despite its presentation of particular conversational manners, this encounter is conceived and executed on a highly abstract and generalized plane. What emerges directly and immediately is the relationship between two persons, not the opposing social conventions that could mediate that relationship. We not only look on the novel essentially from Isabel's point of view, but through James's narrative methods we share her mode of perception, that associated with characters. Time and again we find in James's fiction that the manners he observes and delineates have less to do with the conventions of any particular social group than with the immediate relationship assumed between two individuals, especially as that relationship is qualified by conversational tone and inflection. The more his narratives enmesh us in particular social conventions, as in the later sections of *The American* and *The Portrait of a Lady,* the more he reminds us by image and analysis that we are in the presence of evil.

And this brings us back to the "single small corner-stone" upon which James was to build *The Portrait,* "the conception of a certain young woman affronting her destiny."[17] This destiny is, in Dorothy Van Ghent's phrase, "an investment of the 'free' self in and with the circumstantial and binding past,"[18] but it is a destiny so broadly conceived that circumstantiality and connectedness play a larger role than circumstances and connections. What

[17]James, Preface, *Portrait,* I, xii.

[18]*The English Novel: Form and Function* (New York, 1961), p. 214.

Isabel confronts in the exchange with Madame Merle is not the product of different social practices but, immediately, another kind of individual and, ultimately, the agent of her own destiny to become entangled in circumstance. If Madame Merle anticipates Edith Wharton, Isabel echoes Emerson, in both idea and phrasing,[19] and the basic fable behind *The Portrait* is the immersion of the highly attractive Emersonian character in what James suspected and feared might be "reality." The darkening enclosure that awaits Isabel is primarily the means by which James dramatically accentuates the appealing potentiality of his heroine, just as Madame Merle's urbane and generic "one's self" brings out all the desperate personalism of Isabel's "myself."

The character, then, appears most clearly with all the alluring and radiant hopes it projects about human nature by encountering a world defined and peopled by personages. In a similar manner, innocence emerges most poignantly when it is trapped and destroyed by a fallen world in which innocence itself is irrelevant, as in *Billy Budd*. In fact, the innocence that engages so much imaginative excitement in American fiction is simply the most obvious quality of the Emersonian and Jamesian character, his lack of investment in socially and historically defined attributes. And the fable through which this innocence is tested is a fable of investiture, a tentative entry of the free candidate into a world whose laws and assumptions are inherited, complex, and alien. Whether the testing ground is the series of social arrangements Huck Finn encounters on the banks of the Mississippi, the devious and exacting naval hierarchy Billy Budd enters on H.M.S. *Belli-potent,* the generalized version of Europe to which Henry James exposes his protagonists, or the even more generalized world of the very rich where Fitzgerald's heroes find themselves elated and appalled, what is at stake is how much exposure a character can endure before losing either his integrity or the personal energy by which he can impress his character upon others.

---

[19] Richard Poirier discusses Isabel's (and James's) relations to Emerson at some length in *The Comic Sense of Henry James* (London, 1960), esp. pp. 216-22. He stresses her classlessness, her independence of institutional points of view, and her habit of seeing things in relation to the subjective center of self.

It is the energy at least as much as the integrity that is at stake, for the unconditioned self has a kind of vitality at the center of its appeal. In different ways a group of American novelists of manners at the end of the nineteenth and the beginning of the twentieth centuries accentuated the vitalism, the power of imagining, the inner energy of their characters and measured its dissipation in social activity. This theme is important to Howells, to James, to Dreiser, to Ellen Glasgow, and it is the central conception of F. Scott Fitzgerald. His study of dreams and disillusionment becomes more and more explicitly a study of the dwindling of energy, and the novel of manners becomes in his hands a clinical means of tracing the sources of psychological enervation. With his central characters—Jay Gatsby and Dick Diver—he is less concerned to distinguish personal from social aspects of the self than to differentiate the imagined quality of their desires from the historically and socially conditioned objects to which they fix those desires. It is not Gatsby or Dick Diver who is secretly entangled with society but Daisy Fay and Nicole Warren. In pursuing the incarnations of their best yearnings, Gatsby and Dick lose in social complexity the very energy that allowed them to dream. And this sheer vitality is one of the central qualities affirmed in the American predisposition toward "characters." In its most extreme forms—Jay Gatsby, Dick Diver, Thomas Sutpen—the American character has initially so much of this energy (Emerson's "force") that it can create its own past, its personality, and even its social arrangements. Dick Diver generates the ultimate illusion of a character when his table of dinner guests at the Villa Diana seems to rise a little toward the sky, thereby becoming a new and separate social world for which he himself provides the laws and informing energy and to which his guests bring only "their best selves."

The Circumscribed World and the Diminished Self

For Edith Wharton the table of dinner guests remains firmly, even heavily, fastened to the floor. As Richard Poirier says, in contrasting her stylistic effects with those of James, "the clarity, even to crispness, of Mrs. Wharton's writing indicates a world palpably there in some imposing organization antecedent to anyone's wishes."[20] What interests her is not the free possibilities of consciousness but the conditioned; which is to say that Wharton does not write about characters but about personages. They cannot relate to each other immediately, like James's characters; there is always, in R. W. B. Lewis's words, a third party to the contest. "Her characters tend to be affected not only by each other but also by pressures in the atmosphere; by the more general and pervasive temptations and taboos, by the inexplicable conventions and the vague expectancies of the social setting in this place or that time."[21] And if they lack a character's freedom from social vesture, they also lack his positive quality, the force that can impress itself directly upon other characters and upon the reader. In fact, identity itself is insecure for Wharton's individuals. They find themselves not free agents exposed to a complex trap but creatures of a world so pervasively social that its habits and assumptions determine the very makeup of reality. They put so much time and psychic energy into the casting of their social masks that they are driven to identify themselves with the roles and attributes that others see. Although they have inner natures as well—aspirations, impulses, needs, delicacies, intuitions—their underground selves seem, even to them, unreal. The fable through which Wharton articulates her characters' implication in society involves a release of the second self rather than an investiture of the free self, and the test is not whether social exposure can coexist with integrity but whether, through the emergence of the inner self, integrity can be achieved at all.

Edith Wharton operates, then, under assumptions about the personality quite different from those of such American authors as Howells, James, and Fitzgerald. She also presents a different notion of society. Distinction of person and class comes as no surprise to her characters. Lily Bart knows perfectly well the differences between her set and the people who "lived like pigs," and Newland Archer can tell the exact shade of difference between

[20]Poirier, *A World Elsewhere*, p. 211.

[21]R. W. B. Lewis, "Edith Wharton and *The House of Mirth*," in *Trials of the Word: Essays in American Literature and the Humanistic Tradition* (New Haven, 1965), p. 135.

being any duke and being the van der Luydens' duke. Wharton's secondary characters often have the peculiar substantiality that results from well-observed class traits. Rather than distrust the implicit assumptions behind social nuances, her characters share and utilize them. By focusing on how they interpret their experiences, Wharton not only conveys the implications of social moves and countermoves, the reverberations of small gestures in the cultural context, but she shows how much her characters inwardly participate in that context. This is especially true for the meanings and associations attached to language. To heighten particular moments of conversation, Wharton moves into a character's mind to see what he intends, what he assumes, and how convention determines what he actually says.

If the broad characteristics of American social portraiture I described earlier imply that society is something "out there," a potential threat, Wharton's methods imply something quite different. Society functions as a prison in her fiction, not because the individual, "trailing clouds of glory," has accidentally fallen into it, nor because he is being tested by exposure to its confines, but because he has been born and reared in it; he learns to perceive reality through the bars of a cage. This image of society seems to ally Wharton with her European predecessors, Stendhal, Balzac, Thackeray, George Eliot, rather than with her American ones, and in many ways her literary and historical affiliations are primarily not American. But her version of the opposition between individual and society has a curious component that links her with her own countrymen. In the great European novels of manners the individual may be thwarted and frustrated by society, but he is never so stifled, contained, and diminished as Emerson, Mark Twain, Howells, Fitzgerald, and even James would lead us to believe by their emphasis on the free character. In Wharton's fiction things are as bad for the individual as Emerson could imagine. It is as if the threatening investiture took place at birth and the individual never got the force and freedom that Emerson and James feared he might lose. In fact, society appears in her novels as so intricate and pervasive an enclosure that the individual needs the most adventitious encounters simply to realize how well he is confined. And these encounters—Lily Bart's talk with Lawrence Selden or

Newland Archer's meeting with Ellen Olenska—scarcely give him the force necessary to escape.

Yet although Edith Wharton's protagonists are impaired and trapped by their social orders, they are usually intelligent, sensitive, and sympathetic beings, far superior to their fellow prisoners. Like her own father, as she remembers him in *A Backward Glance*, they are characteristically "haunted by something always unexpressed and unattained," and at every opportunity she accentuates the discrepancy between their outer situations and their inner needs. The major subject of Wharton's fiction is, in fact, precisely how social convention limits the life of the spirit. Thus she needs her baffled, yearning individuals to dramatize and define the constriction itself, and her sympathies are all for these trapped creatures. But she devotes her interest, intelligence, and imaginative energies to the social forms that contain them. And if she often expresses their spiritual cravings in vapid language, it is because her attention is engaged elsewhere.

There is, however, another way of regarding social structures, one that Edith Wharton found especially congenial. Insofar as they contain and stifle the individual, they are static and contemporary. But with her historical hindsight and her solid grounding in evolutionary science, she could see a given society as immersed in change and as the product of former circumstances and gradual adjustments. As Erich Auerbach demonstrates in *Mimesis*, the concept of history as change and development allows a writer to recognize the seriousness and significance of daily life. Because the environment, like the individual, is slowly evolving, the writer represents reality by relating the individual in full specificity to a particular time and place. The substantiality of Wharton's fictional societies and the solidity of her detail result from her awareness of larger historical and social changes going on behind the surface. Such processes as the geographical expansion of fashionable New York and the intrusion of new wealth and new ways of accumulating it give weight and precision to the moral issues of the fiction, and the same processes test the durability of inherited social assumptions. Rather than develop the individual's spiritual possibilities, Wharton amplifies the individual and his plight by attaching both to their larger historical circumstances.

By seeing social structures as parts of a changing environment, Wharton can locate and understand the particularities that give her fiction its solidity. But her view of these structures as the products of distant circumstances and gradual adjustments has more complicated effects. Her ideas about human beings and their social habits were profoundly affected by her readings in evolutionary science. From the principle of natural selection she adapted two crucial attitudes. Whatever in human thought and imagination has survived the ages must represent not only the best but the most congenial to human nature. Similarly, whatever has survived in social structures must be the result of gradual and continuous accommodation to fundamental human needs. Although she recognizes, especially in *The Valley of Decision* and *The Age of Innocence*, that certain forms which answered bygone needs survive as rituals, she treats this phenomenon more as an obstacle to reform than as a reason to doubt the merit of existing structures. In the religious forms of Roman Catholicism and the social forms of the French, Wharton repeatedly praises the accumulated adjustments men have made to live together.

But if social forms have evolved slowly and continuously, human beings have evolved with them, and in the most complicated fashion. Life, as she sees it, "is not a matter of abstract principles, but a succession of pitiful compromises with fate, of concessions to old tradition, old beliefs, old charities and frailties. . . . [Human relations are] a tangled and deep-rooted growth, a dark forest through which the idealist cannot cut his straight path without hearing at each stroke the cry of the severed branch: '*Why woundest thou me?*'"[22] The individual being, then, is rooted in the past and in social tradition through habit, association, and feeling. As his bodily structure has evolved in response to his physical needs and his surroundings, his psychological structure and feelings have developed in close connection with his social activities. These organic metaphors appear in Wharton's writing whenever she voices her great admiration for continuity and tradition. Human thought grows slowly like fruit; ideas must ripen in the mind to attain validity; and culture requires cultivation of "the

[22]*The Fruit of the Tree* (New York, 1907), p. 624.

accumulated leaf-mould of tradition." Unlike Coleridge and Emerson, who use the organic image to describe natural form as an alternative to inherited artificial forms, Wharton uses it to express the natural continuity and development of the inherited forms themselves. By cutting off his complex attachments to these forms, the individual damages his own feelings, severely limits his understanding of human experience, and becomes a danger to others. And when war pulls apart whole civilizations and forces a reversion to bestial simplicity, it leaves man "as a defenceless animal suddenly torn from his shell, stripped of all the interwoven tendrils of association, habit, background, daily ways and words, daily sights and sounds, and flung out of the human habitable world into naked ether, where nothing breathes or lives."[23]

For Edith Wharton, then, it is Emerson's character, not the personage, who is a diminished being. What she calls "the pyramid-instinct"—the slow continuous development through immediate efforts to meet definite objects—has not only formed mankind, social orders, and the monuments of human artistry, but has caused man's "fugitive joys to linger like fading frescoes on imperishable walls."[24] It is only by the individual's connection with the cumulative development of the human race that he and his feelings are enlarged, and this connection is established through inherited patterns that are immediately transmitted by his social order. His fugitive, erratic, and isolated feelings must be made to cohere in actions and words comprehensible to others. His local manners, in the first instance, provide the forms within which this is possible. If, for whatever reason, he is cut off from such forms, he appears inwardly chaotic and outwardly selfish. It is this perspective that makes Wharton a moral and social conservative, especially in her scathing analysis of American life in the 1920s. As one of her characters puts it in *The Gods Arrive*, "We all of us seem to need chains—and wings."

There are, it should be clear, some fundamental contradictions in the attitudes I have described. When Wharton looks on particu-

[23]*A Son at the Front* (New York, 1923), pp. 183-84.

[24]*The Glimpses of the Moon* (New York, 1922), p. 244.

lar social institutions as undergoing change, she sees primarily a deterioration, accelerated after the First World War. When, on the other hand, she praises organic development, she sees social institutions per se as gradually accommodating themselves to human needs. She never juxtaposed these attitudes as acutely as her friend Henry Adams, who surveyed the progression from George Washington to Ulysses Grant and found himself questioning the whole evolutionary hypothesis. A more serious difficulty appears when we consider the relationship between social institutions and the individual. If these institutions take on their importance by the ways in which they limit the life of the spirit, they stifle the individual. And given the basically unsatisfactory social structures Wharton actually portrays, the image of the prison predominates in her fiction. But if institutions intrinsically reflect the lore accumulated through ages of social experience and if the individual life is deeply rooted in them, they are needed to contain self-seeking, ephemeral motives and to give coherence to human activity. In the one view the individual's inner life is the seat of spiritual capacities; in the other, it is impulsive, fragmentary, and mean. This divergence produces one of the most disturbing ironies in Edith Wharton's fiction. Social forms ought to resist the selfish whims of characters Wharton dislikes—Maria Clementina, Bessie Amherst, Undine Spragg—but for such figures conventions simply fail to function. For characters whose aspirations and feelings are attractive, on the other hand, the conventions work irresistibly, not only to fetter the yearning spirit, but to make the characters harmless and ineffectual.

Such attitudes cannot be easily reconciled, and some of Wharton's haunting power derives from the pressure of their antagonism. But the discrepancy between the spiritual and the impulsive aspects of the inner life reflects a disposition characteristic of her writing. Even in its most admirable, unselfish form, she distrusts the promise of personal fulfillment. She expresses this tendency most openly in her sonnet series "The Mortal Lease," in which "one rounded moment" seems to offer all that she can desire in love and spiritual bliss. When the sacramental moment approaches, however, "with tides of incommensurable light," the speaker trembles and covers her face, the moment flees, and its ghost whispers that now she will never know how much fulfillment she might have had.

> Shall I not know? I, that could always catch
> The sunrise in one beam along the wall,
> The nests of June in April's mating call,
> And ruinous autumn in the wind's first snatch
> At summer's green impenetrable thatch—[25]

Here she contents herself with renunciation, in which the potential beauty is realized in muted evocations rather than obscured in the blinding glare of fulfillment; she measures her loss by all that she keeps. Time and again Wharton turns her face from the direct consummation of her characters' longings and renders their meaning with precision and delicacy only in the presence of failure. Furthermore, the baffled aspirations need the very social conventions which cause that failure, for only in the resistance of a larger, more durable order can these fugitive desires be opened to public view and made firm.

It is the long perspective of countless efforts and failures that makes the particular yearning outlast its own brief flare. At her finest moments Wharton conveys simultaneously the immediate pathos and the compensating grandeur of this attitude. One such moment embraces the whole concluding chapter of *The Age of Innocence*. Another occurs late in *The Valley of Decision* when Odo Valsecca, recovering from his defeat as a political reformist, finds in his own experience a confirmation of the theory of history he had learned years before from the abate Crescenti. Instead of judging social structures by comparing them with an ideal state like Plato's Republic, the abate had told him that to comprehend present institutions, one must trace their roots in the past. The real state "was the gradual and heterogeneous product of remote social conditions, wherein every seeming inconsistency had its roots in some bygone need, and the character of each class, with its special passions, ignorances and prejudices, was the sum total of influences to ingrown and inveterate that they had become a law

---

[25] *Artemis to Actaeon and Other Verse* (New York, 1909), p. 44.

of thought."[26] Wharton clearly accepts this analysis. Yet if the
sweep of the theory diminishes Odo's personal failure, the implications of Crescenti's ideas carry us back to particular manners and
people. Human development does not follow the leaps of a
historian's summaries, but occurs slowly and indirectly, accumulating habits and prejudices at each repeated step. The historical
conventions and feelings of each class become laws of thought for
the individual. Both Henry James and Edith Wharton see outward
manners as having an immediate inward equivalent; but for him
they lose their social nature as they pass inside, becoming images,
associations, parts of the mental atmosphere, whereas for her the
forms of conduct become the forms of mental activity itself. In
other words, the individual mind carries in its operations not only
its immediate social arrangements but the erratic progress of a
whole class. Thus, as manners become laws of thought, they create
the nexus of individual and society in Edith Wharton's fiction. But
if the implicit determinism of this idea seems harsh and limiting,
what she says of Odo Valsecca applies to Wharton herself: "the
influence of these teachings tempered his judgments with charity
and dignified his very failures by a tragic sense of their inevita-
bleness."[27] She never relaxes her judgments or releases her finest
characters from the inevitable, but she evinces her compassion for
the whole doomed life of the spirit by her unflinching scrutiny of
manners.

[26] *Valley*, II, 292.

[27] *Valley*, I, 260.

Chapter II

The Mind in Chains
Public Plots and Personal Fables

> But he would lift her out of it, take her beyond!
> That *Beyond!* on her letter was like a cry for rescue.
> He knew that Perseus's task is not done when he has
> loosed Andromeda's chains, for her limbs are numb
> with bondage, and she cannot rise and walk. . . .
> —*The House of Mirth*

WHEN WE THINK of a novelist's characters, his concerns and ideas, his narrators, or more metaphorically, his "world," it is easy to forget that by assembling fragments into useful patterns *after* having read the novel itself, we are representing our experience with it by a static picture. A novelist's world is not only a seemingly coherent collection of persons, groups, places, things, and gestures, but it is a place in which things happen. And our experience with the novel, which occurs not in the space of a world but in the time of a story, has primarily to do with our progressive, dynamic relationship to what is happening—our memories and anticipations, wishes and fears. Novels tell us stories, and stories articulate to us our human condition. Histories tell stories to account for how things did happen; legends, epics, and romances tell stories that show how things would happen if guided by the values and aspirations of a culture. Lawyers publicly assert the credibility of conflicting stories and try to fit them into the sanctioned story-patterns of precedents. We each privately move from the personal past to the imagined future by telling ourselves stories that temporarily satisfy us. We make ourselves and our cultures by telling stories. Whether a novelist assumes that he must tell interesting stories or sets about programmatically to expunge storytelling from his fiction, he implicitly acknowledges that coming to terms with storytelling is central to his business,[1] and

---

[1] See Barbara Hardy, "Towards a Poetics of Fiction: An Approach through Narrative," *Novel*, 2 (Fall 1968), 5-14. This illuminating article shows how novels are often *about* the stories we tell ourselves or dream.

for this reason the components of stories are usually handled with peculiar conscientiousness in novels. The world of a novel, then, is a place in which things not only happen but happen in certain characteristic and significant ways. In his arrangement and motivation of crises, his implicit linking of episodes, his alignment of operative forces, and his manipulation of his reader's expectancies, a novelist reveals his sense of how human life is lived.

As I describe in this chapter the general nature of Edith Wharton's major fiction I am primarily concerned with defining the kinds of stories she tells. Wharton's major subject is the effects of social organization. She measures those effects through the impact of society on the individual, so that thematically her fiction poses the question, How do manners limit the life of the spirit? Such preliminary definitions show us where, within the range of observed and imagined experience, Wharton looks for a story worth telling, but they do not describe the stories themselves. If her fiction involves a conflict between social observation and humanistic commitment, between the assumptions that man is helplessly enmeshed in social habit and that he is responsible to the lofty expectations of Western aesthetic and moral traditions, this conflict must be converted into the dynamic material of narrative. We must be moved through the stories in such a way as to recognize the extent of human entrapment and at the same time to expect something better for the protagonists. Wharton's fiction, then, employs two levels of plot, one overt and public, the other buried, private, and usually fragmentary.

Outwardly Wharton's plots turn on the staple issues of the novel of manners—movement through the classes, courtship, marriage, extramarital affairs, social exclusion or acceptance, and conflict of classes. One of the ways in which novels of manners take society most seriously is by making narrative crises out of issues that are not only recognized but determined by a particular community. While the major plot developments open up the qualities and changes of the central characters, they also dramatize the nature and powers of the social order itself. One way to define the nature of society in a novel, then, is to examine the quality and force of the crucial turnings in the plot. In Edith Wharton's fiction, these major crises are almost entirely social in their thrust. Even the deliberate schemes or intentions of the protagonists themselves often turn on their relations to the social order and thus remain vulnerable to sudden checks in the critical moments. Wharton's overt plots dramatize the movements of the social order and the actions of that part of the protagonist which is socially bound. These plots, as I shall presently show, are deterministic, and they trace the defeat of personal spirit by social power. They reflect the assumptions emerging from Wharton's social observation.

But the overt plots do not account for the momentum of expectation in the narratives. There is a quality of human failure in Wharton's fiction that is far more disquieting than the outward fates of her characters, than, for instance, Lily Bart's progressive loss of social footing. This deeper sense of failure emerges through the defeat or the limited realization of certain anticipations subtly generated by another kind of story than that developed openly. It is the story Wharton wants to tell, and it plays over and over against the stories she actually is telling. The buried fable in her fiction is a story of inward rescue, the release of the protagonist from class-dominated ways of seeing. It begins with the individual in the condition I described in the preceding chapter, bound outwardly and inwardly to the view of reality determined by immediate social habits. Through crises of perception in which he discovers issues of conduct or states of feeling that were formerly invisible, this fable moves the individual toward the release of full psychological and moral insight, making him both an integrated being, in touch with his deeper potentialities, and a member of a more capacious and admirable community. Along the way, of course, such a development sets the protagonist at odds not only with his local society but with himself as well. This buried fable, then, articulates a movement from the world given by Wharton's social observation to the world implied by her moral and personal ideals. Conceived in these terms, rescue is the underlying form of action motivating Edith Wharton's fiction; it converts static issues into stories. By repeated allusions to their potential escape from the socially conditioned, Wharton guides our interest in the destinies of her characters. But she never fully tells the story of inward release; it remains a latent or buried plot, articulating potentialities that in turn shape our anticipations and judgments. The frustration of these possibilities creates that deeper sense of failure in her fiction, measuring the strength of social chains. If the overt plot dramatizes social powers, the buried fable gauges their effect.

Sequences of Fate and the Meaning of Rescue

It is, of course, the overt plots that create the dominant sense of reality in the novels, for they show how things characteristically happen. And there are certain fundamental tendencies in Wharton's plotting that suggest the extent of social power in her narrative worlds. The first overwhelming impression of her fatalism emerges directly from what happens in her fiction; she visualizes her finest heroine, Lily Bart, as living in a story driven from beginning to end by a destructive fatality. But the operative force in Wharton's overt plots is not an abstract fate; it is embedded in the mechanisms and activities of the immediate social order. Her plots involve a dense concentration of public scenes, and the action moves relentlessly between such communal gatherings as if the primary events were taking place among social or historical developments to which the insights and questions of the individual are virtually irrelevant.

One is struck, first of all, with how little time Wharton's characters have to themselves. Even when the protagonists have the good fortune to discover new ways of seeing their experience, they can scarcely reflect on their new insights before being pressed into further complicity with the forward movement of public events. And their rush to keep up with the pursuits of their communities implicates them deeply in a public mode of existence. On the other hand, they cannot safely disregard what is happening in their societies, as Lily Bart learns in losing her hold on Percy Gryce through the interference of Bertha Dorset and in losing her inheritance through the machinations of the "insignificant" Grace Stepney. The agents of social power are constantly active, and they often intrude on the private scene to hasten the errant individual back into his communal place.

As the spaces within which Wharton's characters imagine themselves moving are restricted by the outward arrangements of the societies, so the time scheme through which they apprehend and project their experience is dictated by well-disciplined clocks, well-filled social calendars, and ultimately by a linear and highly regular historical flow which submerges that kind of psychological time in which the moment can become eternity. Unlike such inward novelists as Flaubert, James, and Proust, who in various ways let the subjective experience of the moment create its own sense of time, and unlike such impressionists as Conrad and Faulkner, who allow reconstructed time to emerge in segments so disparate that we question the continuity and uniformity of time itself, Wharton shows through the unquestionable forward movement of her overt plots that any irregular apprehension of time on the part of the individual is peripheral and unreal. Public events surge forward in a time span unaffected by the wills of the characters and impervious to their desires. And Wharton increases this momentum by enclosing the sequences of public activities in larger historical changes occurring within and around the communities themselves. Against this implacable movement, easily felt as the flow of destiny, those private time schemes generated by personal lines of intention are simply dwarfed.

But this continual movement is not always presented directly in the novels, for narrative inevitably proceeds by selection and abridgment, and Wharton's handling of the interstices between scenes suggests another tendency in her plotting. The gaps between a novelist's scenes have a curious power to implicate us, for somehow we must tacitly account for the lapsed time, and to this degree we participate in constructing the narrative movement itself. The nature of this participation in Wharton's fiction is defined most clearly by her strategies for dealing with major narrative divisions. She often closes chapters or sections with relatively private scenes in which characters wrestle with moral difficulties and manage, or so it seems, to evade serious choice by giving in to the strongest apparent pressure. But these evasions are themselves choices, and Wharton measures their personal consequences by beginning the next narrative section, not with an immediate sequel to the choice, but with a scene occurring after a considerable lapse of time. In order to understand the narrative, we must, at least in outline, reconstruct this time segment; beginning with a rule established by the choice itself, we construct a time of determinations and effects, a time measured out by the successive

consequences of the choice.[2] This strategy obviously reinforces
the sense of narrative fatalism, for in looking ahead to events dealt
out in advance, we share the vantage point of the Eumenides.

Striking examples of this procedure occur in the transitions
between books 1 and 2 in each of Wharton's three major novels.
Lily Bart's acquiescence to Bertha Dorset's scheme for a Mediterranean cruise at the end of book 1 in *The House of Mirth* represents
an obvious evasion of her complex difficulties in New York. And
as we see her from outside at the beginning of book 2, we tacitly
fill in the sequence of inevitable compromises and moral indu-
rations that account for the lapse of three months. At the end of
book 1 in *The Custom of the Country* Abner Spragg tries to
maintain his loyalty to a former business associate against Moffatt's
financial scheme and threat to Undine's marriage. When book 2
opens several months later with Ralph Marvell and Undine on their
honeymoon, Spragg is left behind, and we reconstruct for ourselves
his capitulation and the subsequent steps of his abasement. In
The Age of Innocence the same narrative strategy encloses the
central moral decision of the novel, for in the transition between
books 1 and 2 Archer chooses between Ellen Olenska and May
Welland. Having declared his love to Ellen at the end of book 1,
Archer asserts that his new self-awareness makes marriage to May
unthinkable, whereas Ellen argues from Archer's own earlier pro-
nouncements about duty to the community and in particular to
May. It is not certain that Ellen will be able to maintain her

---

[2]This time sense is closely related to that which Georges Poulet ascribes to
nineteenth-century naturalism in his theoretical Introduction to *Studies in Human Time*,
trans. Elliott Coleman (Baltimore, 1956). In earlier nineteenth-century literature, especially in Balzac's fiction, Poulet finds a sense of continuous time, conceived as an
immense causal chain and discovered by tracing the origins of present persons and things,
by analyzing their emergence in time. Behind this genetic process must lie a generative
law, which itself exists outside of time. Poulet sees the naturalists as exiling themselves
from human time, placing themselves in the realm of the generative law and reconstructing time by means of this law. But this time is purely scientific, a time of
determinations and effects, not of causes and origins, and the mechanical application of
a given law generates only what Poulet calls "a dead diagram of time." In Wharton's
fiction, however, the "generative law" is not a scientific formulation of biological and
environmental determinism but rather a configuration of moral inevitability posited by
the conjunction of a given choice and the social world within which that choice is made.
It suggests the same immediate sense of determinism one finds, for instance, in Zola's
fiction, but not the same causes.

sincere reasoning, nor is it clear that Archer can even understand her argument. The arrival of May's telegram, announcing an early wedding, breaks up the deliberation. Book 2 opens at the wedding. Here, instead of accounting for lapsed time by postulating a chain of consequences, the reader is forced into Archer's bewildered sense of what has happened. The very rapidity of the sequence leaves no time to consider whether May's telegram *should* have changed everything again for Archer; the sudden movement shows what power a simple public gesture, here a telegram, can have when backed by a network of social obligations and inward habits. Furthermore, the interval between the telegram and the wedding virtually vanishes, as if the latter were the immediate and the only recognizable consequence of the former. Momentarily, then, Wharton's arrangement of interstices engages the reader in Archer's own illusion that May's announcement eliminates moral choice entirely.

In its immediate implications this narrative strategy does not suggest an external doom hanging over the characters; rather it increases the moral seriousness of their conduct. The sequences begin in private moral dilemmas, and the hypothesized determinations and effects with which the reader fills in the narrative gaps simply measure the personal results of the implied decisions. But the choices made in each case can easily be construed as nonchoices; to the character, the matter seems out of his hands, and even to author and reader the moral agent is not deliberating but following the course of least immediate difficulty. It is the power of social expectancies, reinforced by the pressure of public time, that creates for the character the illusion that only one line of action is even imaginable. Thus, insofar as Wharton's handling of narrative gaps makes us comply in projecting and understanding deterministic sequences, we tacitly acknowledge what personal strength and clarity of insight would be necessary before a character could even contemplate a course of action other than that determined by public pressure. The effect of these narrative gaps is often emphasized, as in the treatment of Archer's wedding, by their coinciding with a sudden passage from a private to a public scene, as if the character's implicit failure to accept his own accountability reduced him to a mere fragment of the communal world.

There are other strategies in Edith Wharton's overt plots, such as a series of contrived coincidences, that suggest more directly the existence of an outside force disposing the events, and this force can often be identified with certain movements of the communal machinery. The most serious and effective of these strategies involves her arrangement of narrative revelations. She constructs her plots so as to undermine the protagonists' moments of expansive meditation by developing earlier the very forces that will frustrate their expectations. As we read of a character's projected freedom and his new patterns of life, it is already clear that these rich possibilities are doomed. The most obvious occurrence of this procedure is in *Ethan Frome*, where the opening scenes take place twenty-four years after the main narrative. Before learning of the crucial four days in Ethan's life, the narrator sees him as the ruins of a once-impressive man. Throughout Ethan's story the reader has two visions of him: that which is unfolding in the chronological narrative of his days with Mattie Silver, a narrative of poignant desires and hopes, and that which the Eumenides must have seen from the beginning, the wreck of a man after more than twenty years of suffering.

In *Ethan Frome*, however, the procedure is extremely simplified; its chief, and virtually its only, effect is to show that Ethan's hopes are doomed before they are recognized, and this is one reason the novel seems harshly fatalistic. Elsewhere the sense of doom is qualified by Wharton's interest in the complex agencies of that doom, the means by which personal hopes are to be thwarted. The story of Ralph Marvell in *The Custom of the Country* illustrates the fuller possibilities of her procedure. Each of his enthusiastic reveries about the future follows ironically on the narration of those other lines of intention that will destroy his plans. His meditations about his son and the salvaging of his marriage, developed at the beginning of book 3, are cast in a hopeless light by the revelation at the end of book 2 that Undine, in collusion with Peter Van Degen, is planning a divorce. Similarly, at the beginning of book 4 Ralph seems to have achieved both independence and personal strength: he has recovered from his illness and from his divorce, he has found peace in his companionship with Clare Van Degen and deep joy in his life with his son, and he has returned with solidity and dedication to his writing. But at the end of book 3 Wharton has already developed Undine's plans to extort money from Ralph for a papal annulment by threatening to take custody of their son, Paul. And Undine's selfish schemes represent only a part of the movement against Ralph's hopes. Her desires activate the larger social machinery of three interlocking classes: the Dagonets retreat in painful silence from the possibility of "scandal"; Clare Van Degen offers monetary assistance that would compromise Ralph by its association with her unscrupulous husband; and Ralph's last hopes rest on his own entanglement with the questionable speculations of Elmer Moffatt. It is the combined working of all these forces that makes Ralph appear a miniscule figure caught in a web of destiny.

Wharton's plotting, then, not only illustrates in outcome the frustration of personal desires but often creates for the reader a doubleness of perspective that makes faith in a character's expectancies impossible, even at the moment of their formulation. We cannot follow the desires and intentions of the protagonists without sensing in the background a steady movement of forces that will shape their destinies. And this effect converges with the other evidences of social power in Wharton's plotting—the arrangement of narrative gaps, the emphasis on public scenes and on the implacable movement between them—to suggest that public time and communal activities define the underlying reality in her novels. It is apparent, then, that the fable of inward rescue is deeply buried beneath a level of happenings that have little to do with the release of the individual from the socially conditioned.

In fact, the powers of a social order reach much farther into the lives of Wharton's characters than the overt plots, fatalistic as they seem, would suggest. To understand the deeper impact of manners in Edith Wharton's fiction, one must look into her ideas about perception, and these in turn reveal the meaning and the potential content of the buried fable. Her characterization is consistently marked by her focus on habits of mind and ways of seeing. Such qualities as the range of a character's susceptibility and the modes of his comprehension virtually define the inward life in her fiction. The seriousness of such issues for Wharton is apparent in the fact that they also govern her projection of herself in *A Backward Glance*, with its emphasis on "magic casements," persons and books that changed her own ways of seeing. This line of interest accounts for her tendencies to juxtapose obtuse and susceptible minds, and to stress the powers of insensitive characters to nullify the delicacies of perception and value to which they are blind.[3]

But her interest goes beyond the delineation and comparison of her characters' worlds of perception; she tries to show why they see, think, and feel as they do. She characteristically shows inward habits as the products of outward ones; social upbringing, in her fiction, not only limits the mind but actually builds and furnishes it. She often formulates this suggestion in a direct or implied metaphor: the individual's mind appears as a house, a theater, a familiar communal space, and his mental activities are rendered through analogy with the social activities characterizing that space. Thus the movements of Undine Spragg's imagination seem adequately represented by the activities in the prairie schoolhouse where she was educated.

The fuller implications of this procedure are apparent in the opening scene of *The Age of Innocence*, where Newland Archer's mind emerges as coextensive with the old opera house. Virtually the entire content of his mind is composed of what is before his eyes, and his inward range of association characterizes the set of communal assumptions that would explain to any New Yorker what he sees and feels. The men in the club box seem interchangeable, not only because they dress and act alike, but because they are quite literally of one mind. And how thoroughly that one mind shapes Archer's own thought is apparent at the end of the scene when he joins the "disgraced" Countess Olenska to demonstrate to old New York his solidarity with his fiancée's family.

Her glance swept the horse-shoe curve of boxes. "Ah, how this brings it all back to me—I see everybody here in knickerbockers and pantalettes," she said, with her trailing slightly foreign accent, her eyes returning to his face.

Agreeable as their expression was, the young man was shocked that they should reflect so unseemly a picture of the august tribunal before which, at that very moment, her case was being tried. Nothing could be in worse taste than misplaced flippancy; and he answered somewhat stiffly: "Yes, you have been away a very long time." [p. 15]

[3]See Blake Nevius, *Edith Wharton* (Berkeley and Los Angeles, 1953), esp. pp. 9-10. Nevius develops at length the theme of small minds entrapping larger ones.

The simple friendliness of Ellen's remark is invisible to Archer, and the reason is clear in Wharton's indication of his thinking. The very categories through which he must try to perceive her have been implanted by the club box. She is a "case," not a person, and the various individuals with whom she actually did play when they wore knickerbockers and pantalettes are visible to Archer only as "the august tribunal." The issue of their talk is not memory but "taste," and within these categories her immediate conduct can only be construed as "flippancy." And more than the vocabulary of Archer's thought has been created by his community; his mental operations themselves are modeled on the activities going on before him. Like the club box across the hall, he is "trying" Ellen's case. Thus the "august tribunal" is not merely associated by metaphor with Archer's mind; for the purposes of this scene the two are indistinguishable.

It is in light of this habitual mode of dealing with her characters' perceptual worlds that one recognizes the force of Wharton's words in *The Valley of Decision*, quoted at the end of the last chapter: "the character of each class, with its special passions, ignorances and prejudices, was the sum total of influences so ingrown and inveterate that they had become a law of thought."[4] She concentrates on how and what her characters can see, because it is here that she can assess the personal impact of manners and their supporting assumptions. The individual mind, in her fiction, develops a structure of values and feelings that corresponds to the informing shape of its social milieu. The contents of the mind— not only the details perceived but the very categories within which they are recognizable—lie, in turn, almost entirely within the purview of the community. Furthermore, a character's inward manipulation of what he sees follows the patterns of activity, that is, the manners, of his class. It is this virtually complete transference between the field of manners and the field of perception that Wharton refers to when she sees the influences of class background becoming a "law of thought."

She measures the cost of this transference in two ways. First, the quality and range of what one can see represent a serious psy-

----

[4] *Valley*, II, 292.

chological issue, especially in regard to what one recognizes of one's own impulses, desires, repugnances, and aspirations. Insofar as an individual's field of perception is also public domain, he does not have a personal identity at all, nor does he have a chance of achieving integrity by mediating between his own needs and his social responsibilities. His inner needs may well conflict with the expectations of his class, but unless he can acknowledge these needs within a configuration of values independent of his society, the best he can feel is a vague discontent. The weakness of will shared by so many of Wharton's central characters can be explained in part by this absence of clearly articulated alternatives between which an act of choice can even be envisaged. So strongly does their sense of what is real depend on the sanction of class assumptions that they can hardly accept their own intuitions and impulses as legitimate objects of consideration. In portraying Lily Bart, Wharton complicates the psychological problem by removing her from even the illusory identity she maintained within her social class. Once Lily has fallen far enough from her original circle to be excluded from the activities she had learned to regard as real, she seems to herself to have no being at all: "If one were not a part of the season's fixed routine, one swung unsphered in a void of social non-existence. Lily, for all her dissatisfied dreaming, had never really conceived the possibility of revolving about a different centre: it was easy enough to despise the world, but decidedly difficult to find any other habitable region" (p. 421). Although Lily's descent moves her steadily to the periphery of her world, she never does enter a circle with a different center; even the millinery shop serves the Trenor world.

The cost of identifying the field of perception with the field of manners can also be estimated in moral terms. One's capacity to see and to recognize issues of conduct determines the extent of one's choices, and in this sense quality of perception is a serious moral matter. In her examination of her characters' ways of seeing, Wharton accounts clearly for the pervasive identification of manners and morals. Communal habits and assumptions create in the individual mind a structure of feeling and perception, and the range of perception determines in turn the scope within which moral choice can be exercised. Thus, unless one develops modes of perception and movements of mind not sanctioned by the immediate social order, one has, properly speaking, no moral life at all; one's conduct and judgment take place in the world of habit.

Facing things as they are is one of Edith Wharton's central values, but one cannot face what one cannot see, and as she presents them, the manners of old New York obfuscate such intellectual and moral honesty. Men of wealth are called "higher citizens," but since the mention of money in social circles constitutes a grave offense, the basis of social prestige is tacitly ignored, and the criteria of social discrimination cannot be fully examined. The combination of hypocrisy and innocence perpetuated by such a code stymies moral deliberation for characters like Lily Bart and Ralph Marvell; since they have no way of understanding the financial operations of men like Gus Trenor and Elmer Moffatt, they cannot assess their own implication in these maneuvers. And the avoidance of financial topics merely illustrates what Wharton sees as an underlying evasiveness in the manners of old New York. By turning its back on suffering and "scandal," the social order prolongs immaturity of mind. Unless his vision is opened, the individual character cannot even choose to confront his moral problems; he simply does not see them. Insofar as the manners of a social order become laws of thought, the individual has neither a personal identity nor a serious moral life. His mind is in chains.

It is this imprisonment that measures the deeper reaches of social power and defines the ground for the fable of rescue. In order to create psychological and moral dimensions in what would otherwise be a purely sociological fiction, Wharton must allow her characters, at least tentatively, to develop new ways of seeing. Without the potential for change, they would not move us. As Wharton investigates the limitations on her characters' minds, she clearly expects them to be larger, more responsible, more individual than they are, and she conveys these expectations by emphasizing the experiences that momentarily can enlarge and open their perceptual worlds. The most significant of these experiences are of three general kinds: suffering, seeing through another's eyes, and participating in class confrontation. These provide the motifs of her buried fable.

The first mode of release seems so obvious as to need little commentary. Of course characters grow in self-awareness through frustration, setback, and failure—these trials are synonymous with one meaning of experience itself. But Wharton lays peculiar stress on suffering, defeat, and loss, almost turning them into virtues. While success blinds her characters, failure often gives them acute powers of analysis. When Wharton needs a flashback to fill in a character's past, she presents it as the character's own retrospection set off by outward defeat, for it is only in such circumstances that the character can *see* what was significant in the past. And some lines from her poem "The One Grief" suggest that Wharton finds as much consolation as waste in the experience of pain: "my grief has been interpreter/For me in many a fierce and alien land/ Whose speech young joy had failed to understand." Through loss or disappointment her characters discover the meaning and value of what they have missed, as they cannot in the anticipation. Thus nostalgia, of a kind related to suffering by its emphasis on personal loss, serves as a major mode of perception for her characters, and indeed for Edith Wharton herself. Newland Archer sees both Ellen Olenska and old New York most clearly as they slip away from him, and "the Atlantis-fate of old New York" is precisely what made Wharton recall and evoke that society so vividly.

The second kind of experience that opens a character's perceptions is more directly related to the notion of rescue, for it involves a potential rescuer through whose eyes the protagonist resees the world and the self. Lawrence Selden, who rightly conceives of his own role as being "the unforeseen element in a career so accurately planned," repeatedly brings on crises of perception for Lily Bart, opening her vision to the baseness of her attempts to gain security in a corrupting society. By preserving interests and points of contact outside the confines of the seemingly brilliant circle in which she struggles to maintain her position, he can offer her a detached vantage point from which to look afresh at her existence: "That was the secret of his way of readjusting her vision. Lily, turning her eyes from him, found herself scanning her little world through his retina: it was as though the pink lamps had been shut off and the dusty daylight let in" (p. 87). As she recognizes here the vacuity of the Bellomont circle, Lily's change in vision becomes a moral crisis. Through adept and almost admirable calculation, she has been pursuing the self-centered, rich bachelor Percy Gryce. At the moment she has brought her pathetic quarry to the point of proposing, Selden arrives, and his mere presence undoes her careful plans by letting her see, and consequently waver at, what she is doing. As Selden's perspective disrupts her scheme with Gryce, his image recurs to change her vision of Simon Rosedale when she has nearly accepted the parvenu's proposal; and when she has resolved to blackmail Bertha Dorset, Selden's presence again alters her attitude toward herself and her actions, thus closing off her last scheme to reestablish herself in an unacceptable world.

The moral crises in Edith Wharton's fiction so often emerge from such changes in perception that the essence of a character's moral development seems to involve the shifts in his ways of seeing. Even when seeing through another's eyes does not immediately change a character's moral perceptions, it may jar him free enough from habitual ways of seeing to open him for later moral development, as when Newland Archer suddenly looks at his New York from Ellen Olenska's distant view. In this context we can see how the anticipations created by the buried fable are effective even when the release does not occur. Wharton's own predisposition to expect greater moral insight from other changes in perception illuminates the comic failures of Undine Spragg. When Undine looks at Mabel Libscomb from what she imagines as Ralph Marvell's vantage point and when she sees her first husband, Elmer Moffatt, through the eyes of her third, Raymond de Chelles, the very fact that she can only recognize the touchstones of class discrimination—the grossness of gesture and the coarseness of phrase—measures her incapacity to develop new forms of moral awareness.

If the experience of defeat and loss or the opportunity of seeing through another's eyes can open new windows in the mind, the third mode of release shakes its very structure. Since the individual's laws of thought initially develop within the social patterns of his class, these inward habits are most effectively broken when the individual encounters another set of manners and assumptions. Wharton repeatedly initiates her characters' moral and psychological growth in the confrontations of differing social orders. The outward conflict of classes, so characteristic of the novel of manners in general, has in her fiction an inward analogue and

effect: the encroachment of new manners on a seemingly stable
class brings about the invasion of unassimilated, alien experience
into the coherent but limited mind of the individual. The outward
jarring of manners serves as both cause and subject matter for the
inward uncertainty, the questioning of what is real. For the individual's sense of reality has been shaped and filled in by the
sanctions of his class, and when he confronts another sense of
reality, visibly sustaining and sustained by another mode of communal existence, he can seriously question his own. He moves,
then, beneath the life of the surface—the life of manners—because
the questions raised by contrasting manners can be resolved only
through an examination of motives, feelings, impulses, and deep-
seated values. As his own moral and psychological lives spring into
being, however, they do so at a terrible cost. Just as the immediate
effect of an outward conflict of manners is to weaken the entrenched class, so the immediate impact of new perceptions and
questions weakens the individual's hold on reality. Many of
Wharton's characters do not survive the assault.

But if the conflict of manners provides a powerful means to
loosen the hold of class habits on the individual's mind, it does not
necessarily liberate him from social determination itself. In fact,
the forces that change his perception are as social in nature as
those that initially formed it. And although he may confront his
problems in his own fashion, his social order collectively faces the
same problems. Wharton's plotting characteristically joins class
confrontations and personal crises in perception as simply two
sides of the same basic phenomenon. Those characters who,
through perceptual trauma, develop something rich and independent in their inward lives — Lily Bart, Ralph Marvell, Newland
Archer — do so at a time when their social orders are threatened
and are beginning to disintegrate.

Despite the importance of the fable of rescue in defining the
expectations through which we follow Edith Wharton's stories, it
is clearly restricted in scope. On the one hand, it is submerged
beneath a sequence of narrative actions that tend to overwhelm
the individual and his interests, and on the other hand, the rescue
itself is rarely completed because the laws of thought bind the
individual too effectively. These restrictions on the fable measure
the power of the social order and the inward helplessness of the

individual, but there are other limitations imposed by Wharton's own conception of rescue itself. The issue for her is never simply liberation from socially created ways of seeing, for freedom in her fiction always suggests anarchy. Rather she conceives of rescue as expanding the framework within which issues and details can be perceived as real. Of course, such expansion enlarges the individual himself, and in two quite distinct ways. The first and more important of these suggests the severe limits of Wharton's very conception of rescue. The sense of self is primarily broadened in her fiction, not by being set off from the social scheme of things, but by becoming attached to larger phenomena outside. The individual sees himself and his life in an ever-enlarging context.

In whatever form a slowly-accumulated past lives in the blood—whether in the concrete image of the old house stored with visual memories, or in the conception of the house not built with hands, but made up of inherited passions and loyalties—it has the same power of broadening and deepening the individual existence, of attaching it by mysterious links of kinship to all the mighty sum of human striving. [*House*, p. 516]

This experience of continuity between the self and the race, between the social order and the cosmos, serves as the goal toward which much of her characters' growth is directed. Rather than free himself as an individual, the character would find his deeper identity as a member of a broader, morally admirable community. It is the immersion of the individual in the wider life of humanity that marks for Wharton his achievement of insight.

But in enlarging his perceptual world by contemplating the continuous span of human experience, what does he see? Odo Valsecca's extensive study of history in *The Valley of Decision* shows him how thoroughly the institutions he wishes to change are rooted in human development. Reading in cultural anthropology reveals to Ralph Marvell and Newland Archer the analogous power of New York's manners and primitive taboos. In other words, when the individual rises above the daily level to survey "the long windings of destiny," he is not so much seeing new things as he is seeing the old things, the manners and assumptions of his class, in a new and more compelling context. His recognition of more complex and general moral issues does not replace his class taboos, it supplements them. The moral side of perceptual growth does not liberate the individual from his class; rather it sanctifies his immediate compliance by referring it to larger truths.

There is, however, a second way in which the individual's world of perception can be expanded in Wharton's fiction. His escape from a class-sanctioned view of reality may put him in touch with his own deeper impulses and needs, may even release a second self with demands so imperious as to sever him from his community. He may consequently enlarge his own being by coming to terms with hitherto unacknowledged potentialities. Even when such larger integration is not achieved, the release of these deeper yearnings makes possible a moving, morally serious antagonism that cannot arise while the mind is in chains—the fundamental conflict of personal needs and communal duties that marks the lives of Wharton's finest characters. I shall return to the complicated relation of manners and psychology in chapter 4.

The Interplay of Plot and Fable

Wharton's overt plots, then, emphasize the power of public crises, the momentum of public time, and the operation of social forces that defeat personal desires. Beneath these plots she formulates the fable of an individual's potential release from socially formed laws of thought, a fable marked by crises in perception that alter the individual's sense of reality. In this configuration of tendencies, Wharton reveals her general estimate of how human life is lived, how things characteristically happen. But this configuration also suggests useful ways of getting at the peculiar qualities of the individual novels. It offers a basis for defining the dynamic aspects of both the social orders and the individual characters. For a society is not only a structure but an all-encompassing mode of activity, and a character is not only a personality but a figure immersed in time by his desires, intentions, and potentialities. By examining the nature and effect of the crises that demarcate the overt plot, one delineates the working powers of a particular social order, its ways of celebrating its values and of confronting its fears. And the same crises define the public self of a character, his ways of responding to social power, and his ways of modulating his explicit, socially oriented intentions when these are thwarted. On the other hand, the nature of the crises in the buried fable illustrates the inward qualities and potentialities of the protagonist, which define in turn the major expectations that guide us through the novel. The three modes of release—suffering, seeing through another's eyes, and participating in class confrontation—need not work in harmony; by emphasizing one or another of these, by shifting or contrasting their effects, Wharton indicates subtle but important distinctions among her protagonists. And finally, through the interplay between the crises in the buried fable and those in the overt plot, Wharton projects the actual dynamic relationship between the personal and the public life. The following discussions of her major novels are based on the questions of how the overt plot characterizes the social order and the public self, how the buried fable defines the inward self, and how the interplay of fable and plot indicates the shifting relation of self and society.

In *The House of Mirth* Wharton created her most dramatic and powerful outward plot. The conflicting lines of intention are unmistakably clear, the emerging crises sharply etched. The social order in this narrative, however dubious its motives, can act decisively, even savagely, giving point to the crises. And these, in turn, are *felt* as powerful because so many of Lily Bart's expectations are attached to the public realm and are thus peculiarly vulnerable to its actions. The dramatic conflict between character and society, however, engages only the public side of Lily, not her inward potentialities, and thus the very power of the overt plot demonstrates how difficult it is for Lily's buried self to emerge.

The powerful fatality of the story is most obvious in the overall movement of the narrative—Lily's progress from class to class. This movement shows how firmly her fortunes are linked to the social order. For although Wharton keeps social prestige explicitly distinct from moral worth, assigning, for example, some despicable qualities to the Trenors and some redeeming qualities to Rosedale and the Gormers, she implicitly equates Lily's social descent with a fall in the most general sense. Lily's loss of well-being, happiness, and security can be estimated publicly through her class affiliation. Even her moral well-being, except in moments of self-recognition, corresponds to her class position: each step downward socially represents greater laxity, more compromises and concessions, more

temptations to evade facts. Furthermore, the three crises consti-
tuting, for reader and character alike, the most devastating blows to
Lily's fortunes are all intensely public, even matter for the social
columns. In rapid sequence Lily is expelled from the Dorsets'
yacht, trimmed of her inheritance, and cut at a restaurant by the
Trenor party. The very force of these crises measures Lily's dependence on wealth and social validity. The general outline of the
plot, then, characterizes a society that hounds the individual and
gradually destroys her.

But this general outline becomes apparent only after one has
read much of the novel; the immediate dynamics of the narrative
involve a series of local plots, and these are generated, not by the
social order, but by Lily's own schemes. She clearly articulates to
herself a sequence of stories, defining her immediate intentions
and aligning her hopes and the reader's. It is her initiatives that
create the immediate impetus of the plot, and the crises occur
when her plans are publicly thwarted. The more energy Lily ex-
pends on these initiatives, however, the less she can develop her
inward self. For the Lily who makes up these stories is as social a
being as Bertha Dorset. Most of her schemes involve the manipulation of men, for marriage (Percy Gryce, Simon Rosedale,
Lawrence Selden) or for financial assistance (Gus Trenor). Lily is
skillful at this art. In fact, she most effectively demonstrates her
personal power, her ability to act rather than simply respond, by
her adept maneuvers with these four men in book 1. Despite the
moral implications, surely her artfulness in personal encounters
helps make her the vivid character she is, as it measures her
pathetic loss of power in book 2. But the cost of this skill is great.
Insofar as these schemes represent Lily's most articulate assertions
of purpose, they attach not only her fortunes but her volitions as
well to the public order. Marriage in Lily's world is primarily a
means of securing social power.

Her personal schemes, then, characterize the social order and
her relations to it, not Lily herself. In fact, her stories project no
change at all in Lily's social place—she must marry and gain wealth
simply to remain where she is. Her position is so precarious, her
social world so threatening, that personal stability involves here as
much cunning, manipulation, and energy as personal advancement

would require in another world, that of Eugène de Rastignac, say, or Julien Sorel. And this implication is stressed by the nature of another series of stories Lily tells herself, those involving her triumph in the Wellington Brys' *tableaux vivants,* her escape on the Dorsets' yacht, her position as social secretary for Mrs. Hatch, her apprenticeship in the millinery shop, and her blackmailing of Bertha Dorset. What are these but desperate efforts to gain time? They do not arise from Lily's desire to become what she wishes, but from her temporary adjustments to circumstance. She is scrambling to keep her hold in a social world that slips away.

The very drama and power of the outward plot in *The House of Mirth* thus draw so much of one's attention that the fable of inward rescue seems tenuous at best, even for the reader. And for Lily herself the public demands on her energy and imagination consume much of the force that could help her realize her interior possibilities. Yet the buried fable does operate in the novel; it is apparent in the fact that the reader expects much more for Lily than she often does for herself. The marked cleavage between Lily's public self and her "real self" corresponds to a split in her inward potentialities. Of the three modes of release making up the buried fable, Wharton stresses two in characterizing Lily Bart—personal defeat and seeing through Selden's eyes—and these not only work in different ways for Lily but also release quite distinct aspects of her inward self. She is a radically fragmented character, and only at the end do the elements of her story coalesce.

The majority of Lily's shifts in perception are brought about by loss, suffering, and defeat, and these interior crises are closely correlated with the crises in the overt plot. Each critical event in Lily's public life creates new interior recognitions, and insofar as this mode of perceptual release is the most common in Lily's inner life, it makes even her inward growth contingent on public activities. Some of these recognitions merely clarify her past for Lily and lead her to project better schemes for holding her position. But more often the inner crises provoked by outward defeat consist of sudden moral clarifications, harsh judgments of her social order and of herself. Although Lily's fine moral sense operates chiefly in the context of failure, at such moments she neither deludes nor spares herself. The keenly devastating formulations through which Wharton reveals both Lily's analyses and their moral limitations suggest that such moments of self-recognition comprise her chief concern in tracing Lily's development.

This aspect of the buried fable, in fact, projects not an escape into new ways of seeing but a liberation of perceptions already latent in the protagonist. Lily's flashes of moral indignation and her sober assessments of her earlier conduct do not emerge from new moral ideas but from a hidden sensibility that bears a curious relation to her social order. Her major judgments of herself, such as those following Gus Trenor's attempt to seduce her and Bertha Dorset's expulsion of her from the yacht, proceed from ethical standards neither different from nor more complicated than those underlying her social order. An unmarried girl cannot borrow money from a married man, with or without the return of sexual favors, and an unmarried girl should not conspire with the amorous affairs of a married woman by distracting her husband's attention. Yet Lily's clear perception and judgment of her actions do constitute a liberation from socially prescribed ways of seeing, because the overt behavior of her class is designed to obfuscate the actual violations of its deep-seated taboos. In practice, the whole social order is slipping away from its inherited moral firmness. Only in the context of unavoidable publicity will the social body move from tacit connivance to collective disapproval. Whenever Lily is released from immediate difficulties, she remains as blind and evasive as her social order. But failure does for Lily what not even the most shocking public crises can do for other members of her class. Lily's defeats not only reactivate dormant public taboos but convert them into vivid personal issues, whereas the moral reversions of her class remain formulary, collective, and often arbitrary as well. In the immediate aftermath of failure, then, Lily personally incarnates the moral sensibility from which her social order is gradually withdrawing, and this sensibility, in unconscious form, accounts for the fastidiousness that makes her hesitate whenever success seems within her grasp. Her very capacity for such illuminating defeat makes her better than the society that condemns her. Thus the inward self released by outward defeat is not strictly personal at all. Indeed, it makes Lily seem like an "old New Yorker" born twenty years too late.

But Lily is, of course, primarily a creature of her own era, and not least in seeming to have inward energies that could be realized only in true independence from the public self. These latent capacities and the expectations they generate are indicated by the other motif of the buried fable, that involving Lawrence Selden's rescue of Lily's "real self." This story operates quite differently from the one suggested in Lily's development through defeat. When Lily looks through Selden's eyes, she not only sees more clearly but she estimates herself and her friends in a new configuration of values and possibilities. His discussion with her of "the republic of the spirit" is, in fact, merely an explication of what has already been happening between them. Every time she sees through his eyes, she detaches herself momentarily from the values and habits of her society, thus becoming a candidate for citizenship in his republic. In other words, Selden's formulation of Lily's potential story entails, at least in theory, her genuine escape from the socially conditioned.

Appropriately enough, the crises marking the development of this story cut across, rather than correlate with, the movement of the main plot. Lily's interludes with Selden appear, even to her, as diversions from her serious actions, blessed moments of release from the schemes of her public self. But in Wharton's narrative worlds, such diversions are dangerous. In the opening sequence of the novel Lily's visit to Selden's apartment is observed by Simon Rosedale, whom she must later propitiate for his compromising knowledge. And the most extensive of these interludes—the afternoon on the hillside at Bellomont—results in the destruction of her schemes with Percy Gryce, both because she loses her own seriousness by comparing him with Selden and because Bertha Dorset poisons Gryce's mind against Lily in retaliation for her taking over Selden. The developments in the buried fable of Selden rescuing Lily are more likely to bring on dangerous crises in the public plot than to emerge from such crises.

But despite the precariousness of her interludes with Selden, during which more threatening difficulties develop in the background, they represent her only experience of inward freedom. Lily demonstrates her release from the socially conditioned by becoming another self—not only clearer in moral vision, but more spirited, more impulsive, and in closer touch with her inward yearnings. In her talks with Selden Lily appears in her most attractive guise, and one can readily believe her when she says that he brings out her real self. The crises in her sense of reality, then, pertain less to the social world than to herself. She learns in Selden's presence to discredit the mask she usually wears and to believe in a better self. But to nourish her real self Lily needs both Selden's presence and his faith in the better self, and it is in this extension of his task as deliverer that Selden fails.

It is not only what Selden can show Lily but what she herself becomes in his presence that makes Selden credible as a possible rescuer. In fact, a good part of our progressive engagement in Lily's story involves the anticipation of their closer union. But the underlying fable that articulates and develops this wish bears a disturbing relation to the overt plot. Throughout book 1 Lily's encounters with Selden appear as lapses from her immediate calculations, but they set up their own dynamic countermovement, especially after the playful discussion of marriage at Bellomont. As Lily's outward difficulties become more complicated, her dealings with Selden seem to be leading toward the only satisfactory resolution of them. After the evening at the Brys' in chapter 12, this implicit story reaches its first crisis; Selden considers proposing to Lily, sends her a note asking to see her alone, and makes the story of rescue explicit to himself:

But he would lift her out of it, take her beyond! That *Beyond!* on her letter was like a cry for rescue. He knew that Perseus's task is not done when he has loosed Andromeda's chains, for her limbs are numb with bondage, and she cannot rise and walk, but clings to him with dragging arms as he beats back to land with his burden. . . . It was not, alas, a clean rush of waves they had to win through, but a clogging morass of old associations and habits, and for the moment its vapours were in his throat. [p. 256]

But this story is no sooner crystallized than it is shattered, for Selden sees Lily leaving Gus Trenor's house at midnight and falls back at once into his class-bound distrust of her. And apart from Selden's note and a newspaper story about his sudden trip to the West Indies, Lily knows of neither crisis. Clearly this fable of rescue exists primarily to manipulate the reader's experience, delineating the hopes that measure what Lily has missed and augmenting the serious effects of social appearances.

At this point in the narrative the latent story of Selden rescuing Lily is almost completely severed from the main plot, and a major element of Lily's character is effectively lost through much of book 2. Only in her final encounter with Selden does Lily's real self reappear to determine the burning of the blackmail letters. And this scene joins the two segments of the buried fable—the release of Lily's latent moral fineness through defeat and Selden's rescue of her inner life from the socially determined. At the end of her life all the possibilities of perceptual growth, moral insight, and inward integrity merge for Lily's final clear vision of what she has missed and what she has saved. "If only life could end now—" she muses, "end on this tragic yet sweet vision of lost possibilities, which gave her a sense of kinship with all the loving and foregoing in the world!" And of course it does. When Selden as Perseus finally comes to her with the word and the faith that will break her chains, his imagined Andromeda is dead.

Although *The Custom of the Country* refers outward to some of the same historical and social phenomena represented in *The House of Mirth*—the Van Degen circle corresponding roughly to the Trenor circle and the Stentorian Hotel world matching that embodied by Mrs. Norma Hatch—the social dynamics of the novels differ so radically as to make the historical correspondence dubious. The contrasts, in fact, serve as a useful reminder that the operative nature of society in a novel is dictated primarily by the kind of story the novelist wants to tell, and only secondarily by the actual dynamics of its historical source. It is clear that Edith Wharton wanted to tell quite different kinds of stories in these two novels, but apart from the obvious contrast of Lily's fall and Undine's rise, it is not so clear what kind of story she wanted to tell in *The Custom of the Country*. And owing to a fundamental change in the nature of the narrative itself, the plot of this novel is much more difficult to describe. In writing *The House of Mirth*, Wharton demonstrated her moralistic bent; human life, both public and private, appears as a succession of sharply delineated crises, significant moments of individual choice or social judgment. The dramatic power of the novel rests on the assumption that the moral life can be analyzed through crucial moments, that it can, in other words, be dramatized. In *The Custom of the Country* the narrative is not punctuated by such emphatic crises, and there are no single episodes of such dramatic intensity as Lily's propitiation of Rosedale at the Van Alstyne wedding or her ejection from the Dorset yacht. The moralist in Edith Wharton has been superseded by the sociologist, and the crises in the relation of self and society have given way to contrasts in the social orders themselves.

In an obvious break from the assumptions underlying *The House of Mirth,* Wharton says here that "the turnings in life seldom show a sign-post," and clearly the turnings in Undine's story are more gradual and less marked than those in Lily's. If one isolates, for example, the ostensibly public crises that would mark the rudimentary outline of Undine's story, one sees immediately the characteristic narrative choices that define the focus of this novel. All of these crises—her engagement and marriage to Ralph Marvell, the birth of her son, her divorce, her marriage to Raymond de Chelles, her second divorce, her marriage to Moffatt—occur in the interstices between chapters, and the narrative itself develops the contrasts of value and behavior *within* the given state of Undine's progress. What drama there is tends to be illustrative rather than critical. Little is changed in the dramatized scenes themselves; they simply emphasize continuing conflicts in feeling, or they reveal those changes in relations that have been developing imperceptibly.

When one appraises this lack of dramatic development by reference to Wharton's canon that the writing of good fiction consists in "disengaging crucial moments from the welter of existence," one suspects that the phenomenon represented in *The Custom of the Country* is somehow intractable, that the crucial moments cannot be isolated. What Wharton seems to be confronting here is public and personal life without issue. Everything in this novel seems to dissolve: standards of conduct, scales of value, the meaning of language, rituals of transition—all the intellectual and social demarcations that distinguish one thing, one time, or one person from another. The most obvious case in point is the institution of marriage. But on a larger scale the social orders that should provide the sanctions enforcing this institution are themselves incapable of decisive control. Exclusion and communal disapprobation—those public forms in which a social body expresses its collective judgments and asserts its cohesion in the face of threats to its values—appear in this novel as formal gestures devoid of significance. It simply does not matter to Undine Spragg, or even to Upper Fifth Avenue, that Ralph Marvell's family in Washington Square is shocked at the very mention of divorce. When Undine loses her position in New York by divorcing Ralph and is cut at the Opera House, the ostensibly critical scene lacks the force of comparable scenes in *The House of Mirth*. The uncertainty of communal response suggests that her loss of place will be only temporary, and the implication is that marriage, divorce, and social acceptance do not mark major differences for the individual. Although Wharton delineates important contrasts in the values and behavior of a wide range of social orders—Apex, New York's West Side, Upper Fifth Avenue, Washington Square, European watering places, Paris, the French rural estate—the distinctions emerge rather as a subject for speculation than as a source of decisive conflict over comprehensible issues. It is not the forms and activities of the social orders but the authorial commentary itself that conveys judgment and discrimination in *The Custom of the Country*. The book involves more intellectual comedy than social drama, and one of Wharton's underlying perceptions in coming to terms with Undine's story is that it lacks the material for dramatic significance.

There are two related phenomena in this novel that account for the dissolving of comprehensible issues. The first is the dominance of money. Although money figures significantly in the social activities of all Wharton's novels, nowhere else does it so exclusively determine the outward transitions. The crises in Ralph's marriage to Undine repeatedly turn on financial considerations, and each of their moral problems seems resolvable by money. Similarly, the public crises marking the movement of the larger social world are precipitated by shifts in fortunes. In other words, the crises in the overt plot do not engage deep communal or personal responses to what is esteemed or deplored; money mutes the crises by dissolving those collective feelings that could emerge in outrage or approbation. The second phenomenon is determined by the kind of story Wharton is telling. As the immediate impetus of the plot in *The House of Mirth* is created by the plans of Lily's public self, so the impetus here comes from Undine's social desires. But whereas Lily's plans meet public opposition in emphatic crises,

Undine's create public crises in which others must adjust to her wishes. Lily's disappointments and reassessments emerge from her failures; Undine's emerge when she has taken stock of her successes, and her discontent almost immediately provokes a new public crisis. Wharton is not only telling here a story of social ascent but dramatizing the ravages of the nouveaux riches, and such a story presupposes the vulnerability of the supposedly dominant social order. Thus Undine shapes the plot of her novel as none of Wharton's other characters can, and the potentially dramatic meeting of self and society disappears in the spectacle of personal triumph.

It is, however, not only the assumptions about the operative social orders that blunt the force of narrative crises here, but Undine's own nature as well. There is nothing in Undine corresponding to the cleavage between Lily's social ambitions and her deeper impulses and repugnances; all of Undine's yearnings align her with a public existence as all of her perceptions are shared by a social class. Thus neither of the antagonisms that sharpen the issues of Lily's story—that between the social order and the public self or that between the public and the buried selves—appears in Undine's story. Again, this phenomenon could be attributed to the kind of story being told, but not entirely. It is easier to dramatize the widening cleavage between self and society in a story of social decline than in a story of accruing success, and as the protagonist more readily questions his ties to an inimical than to a sustaining reality, the story of social decline can readily dramatize a splitting of the self as well. But novels of manners have often dealt with ascent through the classes, and a conventional mode of irony has been developed within the genre to preserve the distance between individual and class. As one sees in such stories as those of Julien Sorel, Eugène de Rastignac, and Silas Lapham, the social ascent characteristically entails a moral deterioration, which often becomes perceptible, at least in the end, to the protagonist himself. This mode of irony does not operate in *The Custom of the Country* because movement through the classes does not change Undine in any serious way. Although Wharton emphasizes another kind of irony in showing Undine's success to be perfectly empty, it is clear that social triumph costs Undine nothing, morally or personally. She may gain power to effect her will, thus looming larger as a threat, but Undine's moral predisposition is no worse at the end than at the beginning, and her estimate of herself remains impervious to experience.

Clearly, then, the materials of the overt plot in *The Custom of the Country* are intractable, at least within the framework of Wharton's concerns for public and personal issues. It is, of course, possible to dismiss the book as mere social satire and Undine as pure caricature—in other words, to see Wharton as simply releasing her irritation with the "invaders" of old New York. But such a reading accounts for neither the power of the novel, the disturbing force of Undine as a character, nor the perplexing relationship of author and heroine. And it ignores the predispositions of Edith Wharton's art. This is an art of discrimination and disjunction; it exploits observable conflicts in behavior, value, and intention. She gets hold of her stories by locating those social and personal issues that can produce dramatic encounters, outward resistances, and morally significant crises. These habits pertain not only to her ways of telling stories but to her ways of thinking and analyzing as well. And the expectations fostered by these habits govern one's experience of *The Custom of the Country*. That is, this novel not only does not show outward conflict over comprehensible issues but makes it painfully clear that conflict is being dissolved, that potentially dramatic issues are being blurred. Similarly, Wharton not only shows little of importance happening within Undine herself but makes it portentous and disquieting that so little happens. It is the buried fable that puts such expectations into this novel, creates its strange power, and makes one question what it is really about. For while one follows what is happening, one is forced to recognize what is *not* happening.

The buried fable, then, does not primarily characterize Undine's deeply personal nature, as in the stories of Lily Bart and Newland Archer, but instead introduces a set of expectancies that measure what both Undine and her social world lack. Wharton not only describes and dramatizes what Undine is, but projects into the novel what she wishes her heroine to become, thus making a major narrative issue out of Undine's failures. This in itself makes Undine much more problematic than a mere caricature, but by a curious split in the implications of her buried fable, Wharton further complicates her heroine, making her virtually human, and calling into question the very norms of the novel. The two modes of perceptual development Wharton exploits in characterizing Undine are the witnessing of class contrasts and seeing through another's eyes. As in the story of Lily Bart, the motifs of the buried fable do not function in harmony, nor do they move toward the same goal. But in Lily's story the differing implications of personal defeat and seeing through another's eyes characterize a split in the heroine's inward potentialities, a split that can be imaginatively reconciled, at least at death. In Undine's story the disjunction in the buried fable reflects instead the fragmentation of Wharton's own attitudes, and there can be no reconciliation.

It is Undine's constant movement from class to class, her observation of many discrepancies in manners, that provides the largest field in which the story of inward release could develop. And the potentiality is emphasized by the fact that in certain ways Undine has a good eye and a capacity for discrimination. Each time she enters a new *monde*, she quickly notes the prevailing modes of gesture, locution, and appearance and shifts her own behavior to correspond with the "shades of demeanor" she observes. But there is a discrepancy between what Undine sees and what Edith Wharton tells us she sees. Undine observes countless particularities of dress, mien, and tone, whereas Wharton characteristically summarizes the details in an abstract phrase—"refined," "subdued," "allusive." Undine sees what she can imitate, outward manners. Wharton's formulations blend patterns of behavior with their moral content, which is derived from the habits of feeling, judging, and valuing within a social order. What Undine *ought* to be seeing, then, is an integration of behavior and value within the coherent traditions of a class, and Wharton consistently presents these alien traditions as more attractive than Undine's. In other words, Wharton does not assume, as Howells, Balzac, and Stendhal at least suggest, that a social rise is likely to produce a moral fall. Quite the opposite. She sees Undine's climb as a series of splendid opportunities to develop new ways of seeing and to discover deeper and more durable values. The thrust of the novel is that Undine wastes all these opportunities, that she remains untouched.

This frustration of potential development is also indicated by the explicit motif of rescue. Using the same allusion as Selden, Ralph Marvell imagines himself as Undine's deliverer: "he seemed to see her like a lovely rock-bound Andromeda, with the devouring monster Society careering up to make a mouthful of her; and himself whirling down on his winged horse—just Pegasus turned Rosinante for the nonce—to cut her bonds, snatch her up, and whirl her back into the blue . . ."[5] The inflation and irony here are reminders of Ralph's ineffectuality, but even if he could help Undine as he imagines, what would his rescue do for her? Exactly what her growth through class ascent would do: not liberate her from the socially conditioned but encourage insights and feelings based on a more satisfactory social order. As Ralph himself recognizes before he transfigures himself as Perseus, what he is really trying to do is not to rescue her from social submersion itself but to protect her from a particular class that he abhors—"to save her from Van Degen and Van Degenism." And each time Ralph recognizes Undine's failures, what most disturbs him is not her general moral deficiencies but her specific obtuseness to the delicacies that inform his own class. He wants her to see what Wharton wants her to see, and Undine refuses to look through his eyes.

In fact, the actual experience of seeing through another's eyes in this novel works in an entirely different way. Wharton presents here a group of characters who are remarkably dependent on one another. They cannot fall back on inward strength, nor can they rely on that personal force which is supported by the beliefs of their own social orders. When Ralph discovers the inadequacies of his class habits, their irrelevance to his present experience, he illustrates the overall weakness represented in the novel, the weakness that leaves money as the primary determinant of outward crises. These characters need their own beliefs constantly reinforced by the people around them. Thus instead of opening new windows in the mind, the experience of seeing through another's eyes either provides such reinforcement or makes the character confront a wall of indifference or scorn. The crises in the sense of reality do not directly offer an alternate reality; they simply demolish the existing one, as is shown by the tumbling of Ralph's rites and sanctions in the face of Elmer Moffatt's blunt indifference.

---

[5]*The Custom of the Country* (New York, 1913), p. 84. Subsequent references to this edition will appear in the text.

The same pattern appears in Undine's experience, but with variations that create the central ambiguity of the novel. In her case what is real is never a set of habits, beliefs, or feelings, but a set of objects and activities to be desired. It is natural for her that "reality" should change, and the key to her transitions is her lively awareness of scorn or indifference. Whenever she sees that someone worthy of recognition does not care about what she herself wants or has, her first thought is that such a person must know of more and better things to want, although what she sees is the indifference, not the alternate values creating it. This pattern appears in each of Undine's initiations into a new class. But it can also produce reversions of desire, and when it does, it virtually relocates the normative emphasis of the novel.

Clearly the latent story of inward growth through class ascent is unsatisfactory in essential ways. By its frustration it measures Undine's failures and blindnesses, but what would Undine be if she *could* fulfill the expectations of this story by learning to behave and feel as if she were raised in Chelles's family? If part of Wharton's characteristic buried fable involves the release of a deeper and truer self, surely the protagonist cannot simply be severed from her past. Throughout most of the narrative Undine's past in Apex emerges merely as a source of comedy, but when she faces her old rival Indiana Frusk, who has succeeded in marrying the wealthy James Rolliver after a double divorce while Undine has failed at the same ploy with Peter Van Degen, something new enters the narrative: "all Undine's superiorities and discriminations seemed to shrivel up in the crude blaze of the other's solid achievement." The inward crisis works backward, measuring Undine's present self not by what she can become but by what she was. The bolder, more authentic representative of Apex is calling into question all the refinements that Undine has, with effort, acquired.

Implicit in this crisis is the suggestion that Indiana Frusk reawakens a powerful self in Undine that has secretly resisted all her superficial acquirements. This suggestion is made explicit in Undine's relationship to Elmer Moffatt. Despite his vulgarity and swagger, he stirs "the fibres of a self she had forgotten but had not ceased to understand." When he unexpectedly arrives to appraise the Chelles tapestries during the sharpest stage of Undine's discontent over her French marriage, he brings on the major crisis of her inward life:

"Well, that sounds aristocratic; but ain't it rather out of date? When the swells are hard-up nowadays they generally chip off an heirloom." He wheeled round again to the tapestries. "There are a good many Paris seasons hanging right here on this wall."
"Yes—I know." She tried to check herself, to summon up a glittering equivocation; but his face, his voice, the very words he used, were like so many hammer-strokes demolishing the unrealities that imprisoned her. Here was someone who spoke her language, who knew her meanings, who understood instinctively all the deep-seated wants for which her acquired vocabulary had no terms; and as she talked she once more seemed to herself intelligent, eloquent and interesting. [p. 536]

He dismisses all that Undine has learned to value, and he succeeds not only because of the tangible evidence of his power but because he can appeal to Undine's buried self. And if his blunt, vulgar speech challenges the equivocation of Undine's imitated language and feelings, it is at once so vivid and exacting as to upset the normative language of the narrative. Presumably the last clause here is sarcastic, but in the context of Moffatt's speech, the words "intelligent, eloquent and interesting" seem too pale to convey the standards by which we are to judge Undine. They emerge, in fact, not as the normative language but as evidences that Undine's "acquired vocabulary" is indeed inadequate to her feelings. In other words, the effect of this crisis of recognition is ironically to affirm the self that Undine has forgotten. Two chapters later she begins reconstructing this self by indulging in her most energetic memories, those concerning herself and Moffatt in Apex. The contrast between the defiant young Moffatt and the contained, subdued atmosphere of Saint Désert makes the assumptions of the Chelles family seem not only stifling to Undine but vapid in themselves. In the context of this development, it is peculiarly satisfying to see Undine return to Moffatt.

In fact, the brilliantly conceived conclusion of *The Custom of the Country* is satisfying in many ways, perhaps too many. First of all, one enjoys a detached amusement at the overall fitness of things. It is aesthetically pleasing to see Undine come full circle;

the form expresses and seals her fixity of character. And there is a moral pleasure as well, for even though the social sanctions in the novel are too weak to allot Undine the outward punishment she deserves for her treatment of others, a cooler, more discriminating justice has rewarded her worst inclinations. Among boundless acquisitions, she leads an empty life. Finally, there is the generic satisfaction of comedy: in a novel filled with marriages, Undine's union with Moffatt is the real and conclusive marriage, the outward form by which both characters are judged and properly placed. It is so fitting a marriage as nearly to resolve the characters into the abstract conditions they embody: endless erratic desire is joined with boundless means for gratification. This union expresses Wharton's judgment not only of Undine but of the world she inhabits, a world in which every limit tends to dissolve. When the final human boundary between desire and its object is eradicated, the pleasure of desire itself is gone.

But this is a novel, not a morality play, and Undine's marriage to Moffatt is satisfying in ways that do not allow such speculative disengagement. The marriage not only judges but completes a character, and we have seen enough of Undine to take a simply human interest in her. She is, finally, a remarkably vivid character, too vivid to be resolved into a moral or social condition. Although she misses all her ostensible opportunities, she finally achieves a kind of integrity. Her marriages to Ralph and to Raymond are, after all, nearly as false to her nature as to theirs; Moffatt brings out her real self. Thus the two variants of the buried fable—the improvement through class ascent and the release of a deeper self—create opposing expectations and conflicting bases for judgment. Superficially, the difficulty is minimized by the fact that Undine's real self is no more attractive than her acquired mask, but what finally does Wharton want her to be? Despite its brilliant comedy, *The Custom of the Country* remains her most perplexing novel.

In *The Age of Innocence* Edith Wharton discovered a subject that all the resources of her narrative art could only enrich. Her skill at managing outward crises converges here with a communal order in which such crises engage feelings and habits that reward complex elucidation. And Newland Archer has both the socially derived intricacy and the inward potential that allow her to explore fully the story of interior release. Indeed the buried fable is so extensively developed in this novel that it virtually replaces the public narrative as the overt plot of book 2, submerging the movement and crises of the public order but not diminishing their power. And this full development of the buried fable reveals the limits of rescue in Wharton's fiction.

The peculiar qualities informing the public world in *The Age of Innocence* are immediately apparent when one compares the outward crises here with those in *The House of Mirth*. In the earlier novel there is an element of arbitrariness in the public crises, a constant suggestion that a larger fate, inimical particularly to Lily Bart, disposes the outward action. This sense arises in part from the fact that such disproportionate force can be exerted by a few malicious individuals, without any check from the larger considerations of communal interest. But the real source of arbitrariness lies in the discrepancy between everyday tolerances and deep-seated taboos. This discrepancy does not diminish the power of exclusion or disapprobation in a crisis, but it makes the critical moments erratic, and because the implied social judgments do not reflect underlying certainty of communal interest, exclusion becomes wantonly harsh, virtually absolute. In *The Age of Innocence*, on the other hand, one is impressed by the air of intelligence informing social action. Malicious individuals can provoke public crises, but in the critical moments they are put in their places by tribal authority, which operates for the stability and immediate interests of the community. Furthermore, the daily behavior and the deeper values of old New York are in close enough alignment so that when serious crises arise, the collective will is neither arbitrary nor uncertain; it locates the danger precisely and moves to counteract it gracefully. (The response to Beaufort's banking failure does form an important exception to this principle, but it clearly emerges *as* an exception, a hint of the coming dissolution of old New York itself.) Of course, the "intelligence" of old New York covers only a quite limited range of moral, intellectual, artistic, and economic experience; this is the problem that goads Archer into rebellion. But within its range, which has to do rather with the coherence of a class than with the possibilities of humanity, the communal intelligence is extraordinarily shrewd at discerning subtle deviations in feeling and conduct from its central values. Thus, when a conflict emerges, the issues are clear, and the crises in the struggle appear as moving confrontations between two wills, one communal and one personal, not as the hammerblows of fate.

To dramatize old New York and its impact on the individual, Wharton needed a special kind of story. Unlike *The House of Mirth*, with its overt plot of Lily's fall, or *The Custom of the Country*, with its overt plot of Undine's ascent through the classes, *The Age of Innocence* tells the story of a love triangle. Stories of an individual moving through the classes are virtually generic to the novel of manners, and as the very possibility of Undine's rise illustrates, they often assume social orders in transition. The story of a love triangle can be told in a wider variety of ways or genres, and instead of plotting an individual's qualities against a series of social orders, it tends to focus directly on personal psychological matters, leaving at best an implied relationship to a specific community. Wharton varies the thrust of the story by making the relationship to the community explicit and central and by predicating the psychological development on the quality of the social order. She is, of course, interested in what shape Archer's ties to May and Ellen can take and what they will make of him, but she is at least equally interested in how this perennial human difficulty is handled by a particular society. It is on this issue that she dramatizes the functioning qualities of old New York.

In book 1 the overt crises and the issues impelling the narrative involve, for the most part, a problem prior to those of the love triangle itself but crucially related to them, the problem of Ellen Olenska as an outsider appearing in the midst of a provincial community. The first question her presence raises is whether she should be accepted, and this question precipitates three public crises. The first is at the opera, when her appearance in the Mingott box scandalizes New York and Archer instinctively feels that he has to hasten the announcement of his engagement to lend family support to the Mingotts and Wellands. The second is more serious. Lawrence Lefferts leads a collective refusal to attend the Mingott dinner welcoming Ellen, and Archer and his mother persuade the van der Luydens to exert their ultimate social authority. They do, in a characteristic manner. They give their own dinner, inviting, and thereby incorporating, Ellen but also pointedly including Lefferts, thus tacitly reproving his presumption but also keeping him firmly within the social order that now includes Ellen as well.

Sillerton Jackson instigates the third crisis by trying to create a scandal over Ellen's attendance at one of Mrs. Struthers's Sunday entertainments. Again the van der Luydens restore order by gently reminding Jackson that they like the Countess Olenska and by explaining to Ellen old New York's judgment of Mrs. Struthers. In these crises we see the elemental workings of tribal will. The difficulty of accepting a newcomer is apparent in the fact that it requires two interventions of the highest authority to give Ellen a relatively secure place. But we also see here a social order that does not depend solely on the harshness of exclusion for its coherence; it has possibilities for integration and correction *within* the society itself.

Ellen raises a second difficulty by her desire to divorce her cruel husband and regain her personal freedom. Again the problem is public and critical; it involves old New York's taboo against divorce. A Mingott-Welland family council determines that Ellen must give up her plan but fails to persuade her, and another of old New York's mechanisms of authority is brought into play—the intricate connection of social class and the law. Under the cloak of "legal" advice about the "complications" of the case, the family can indirectly exercise its authority, and in this instance Ellen agrees to give up divorce and the crisis is shunted aside.

The interesting thing about this public development is Archer's role. From the outset of the narrative he has been a central figure in the public crises, acting directly, out of loyalty to May in the first instance, and indirectly in engaging the authority of the van der Luydens. Now he again plays the central and most difficult role of legal adviser to Ellen, that is, as mediator between her and the family-community. The family's naming of Archer seems to rest on two fairly obvious considerations: he can be trusted, and they know that Ellen likes him and respects his judgment. But these evident motives, assuming the family's alignment with Archer and its primary concern with Ellen as a wayward outsider, do not account for their informing Archer peremptorily through his legal superior, nor do they account for his consternation, his immediate sense of entrapment. The family seems to have surmised that the very qualities giving Archer persuasive power over Ellen—his presupposed abilities to talk with her sympathetically—represent in themselves another kind of threat, his own divergence in feeling and conduct from the assumptions of the community. By approaching Archer himself through the machinery of the law, then, they remind him of his primary obligation to his own community and to May, show him that they know he has a relationship with Ellen outside New York's sanctions, and transform this relationship into the highly official one of family lawyer and client.

Of course, there is still no direct suspicion, even on Archer's part, that he is falling in love with Ellen; the family's machinations simply attempt to restrengthen his alignment with the community. But the crisis over Ellen's divorce marks the transition between the relatively simple problem of dealing with an outsider and the larger problem of governing Archer's relationship to that outsider. The maneuver making him a legal adviser illustrates the characteristic means by which the collective order attempts to control this relationship, not immediately by destroying it, but by sanctioning it in an official form recast from potentially illicit materials. Thus May explicitly asks Archer to help keep Ellen happy while the Wellands are in Florida, thereby converting into an open duty what he would have done as a secret pleasure. And at the final dinner the guests happily support the public relationship between Archer as host and Ellen as guest of honor.

These measures, however, damaging as they are to what is best between Archer and Ellen, do not suffice. When Archer suddenly leaves his office and dashes to Florida to see May, she and her family know that matters are more serious. Even New Yorkers in love do not behave so precipitously. Why, after displaying her generosity about "another woman" (albeit the wrong one) and convincing Archer that they should not hasten their wedding, does May turn around without telling him and get family support to marry Archer early? And why does she find it necessary to telegraph Ellen about the change? At first reading, these facts seem fortuitous, more of Archer's bad luck with Ellen, but in retrospect they become evidence of the boldest maneuver of family and community to keep Archer in line by sealing his union with society in the most solemn of rituals. As the engagement was hastened to avert a crisis over Ellen's appearance in New York, the wedding is moved up to avert a crisis in Archer's relationship to her.

Wharton's narrative selection in dramatizing the wedding itself shows its underlying meaning. She devotes seven pages to the scene with Archer waiting on the chancel step and only half a page to the appearance of May and the ceremony itself. Archer, arrayed in all the vestments that subsume him in an ancient rite, standing passively before the eyes of the entire community, which is assembled in turn to judge and to celebrate—this is the tableau Wharton emphasizes as containing the intent of the ritual; it surprisingly resembles Hester Prynne on the scaffold. And in contrast to his best man, who says, *"She's here!,"* Archer cannot see May as a person until she is at his side; he sees "the white and rosy procession" and "the vision of the cloud of tulle and orange blossoms floating nearer and nearer." From the perspectives of both narrator and groom, this is some awesome ceremony having primarily to do with Archer himself.

The wedding scene marks a major shift in narrative focus. In the most ritualized public scene in the novel, we suddenly find ourselves looking at Archer's mind itself as the dramatized setting for the major action, and this new focus is retained for most of book 2. The public crises now take place behind the scenes, a narrative strategy corresponding to Archer's severance from the concerns of the community. Count Olenski's request that Ellen return to him brings into the open the family's desire to be finally rid of a vexing problem, but in this council they acknowledge, by excluding Archer, how grave a problem he himself has become, and he learns of the deliberations only indirectly. As long as Ellen stays in Washington, however, she can be tacitly ignored.

It is Ellen's return after Mrs. Mingott's stroke that provokes open dismay in New York and brings on the convulsive movement that leads to her ejection. The family and the community now assume Archer is having an affair with Ellen, and they use all their collective machinery to stop it. The Mingotts and Wellands persuade Mrs. Mingott to give Ellen an allowance to live abroad independent of her husband. And even May's pregnancy is converted from a natural phenomenon to a social gambit by her telling Ellen before it is verified. The celebratory dinner, then, is both "a tribal rally" to eliminate a kinswoman and "a conspiracy of rehabilitation and obliteration," another formal seal on Archer's union with May and his community.

The outward plot of *The Age of Innocence* thus involves the communal manipulation of a love triangle. The activities that

dramatize old New York are subtle, complicated, and nearly constant, as opposed to the harsh, direct, but intermittent expressions
of community in *The House of Mirth*. Instead of exclusion or
overt castigation, the public crises move toward rehabilitation,
toward the absorbing of the deviant personality into a communally
sanctioned role. If the society in *The House of Mirth* is more
obviously threatening, the power of old New York is more pervasive and intricate. Instead of initiating projects for his personal
advantage, the individual here finds himself playing a part decreed
by his community or his habits, Ellen's champion or her legal
adviser, May's eager fiancé or her bewildered groom.

But because personal gambits are rare in old New York, Archer's
occasional formulation of his own lines of intention shows a
genuine divergence from his community and expresses impulses
that have no social sanction whatever. Thus his pursuits of Ellen
to Skuytercliff and later to Boston, and his projected flights to
Washington and to Europe, arise from his desperate longings to
be with Ellen and to escape his social enclosure. These ventures
outwardly chart the development of his inner life. The trip to
Skuytercliff arises from pure impulse, and only later can Archer
see in that impulse something of his buried self. The trip to Boston,
on the other hand, expresses his conscious need for a change. He
now understands his own frustrations, and his longing for Ellen
involves a potential inward satisfaction that is not an obvious
threat to his community. When Archer plans to follow Ellen to
Washington and then to Europe, however, his motives have changed.
His more overt sexual passion now appears incompatible with the
balance of loyalty and fulfillment achieved in Boston. In fact, his
feelings are out of control, and he knows it perfectly well. Not
accidentally, the trip to Boston coincides with the only period of
quiescence in the public activity, whereas the later projected flights
coincide with the most extensive maneuvers of family and community to control Archer and to eliminate Ellen.

The release and expression of these impulses, of course, make
up part of the buried fable in *The Age of Innocence*, and here the
fable is closely correlated with the overt plot. In fact, it is the
possibility of Ellen's liberating certain members of the tribe from
their own taboos and sanctions that constitutes the underlying
threat giving rise to the outward crises in the novel. That is, Ellen's

potential role as the agent of rescue is in part perceptible to the community. In the buried fable this role is a promise, not a threat; she can mediate between Archer and a larger world. But in the overt plot she appears dangerous, and Archer's entanglement in this plot forces him to mediate between her and old New York. Ironically, it is this official role that makes him aware of his chains and thus allows his inward release to begin, for such mediation involves more than the family council had anticipated.

In the first place, Archer's role requires of him that he understand both Ellen and old New York. He must examine his own conventions with an eye to justifying them and making them compelling to a foreigner, and at the same time he must try to understand Ellen well enough to see his sanctions from her perspective. Given Archer's sympathetic intelligence, his official role itself sets his imaginative and analytic faculties to work in such a way as to begin his release into a larger moral and social view. Thus Ellen needs to make only the most casual observations—that the great influence of the van der Luydens, for example, may simply arise in their making themselves rare in society—to make Archer see New York as if through the wrong end of a telescope, "disconcertingly small and distant." That is, Ellen's personality and behavior are not yet at issue; her mere presence in New York and its social complications suffice to bring on Archer's initial shifts in perception. He shocks himself by his own imaginings and his own analyses, and he is especially vulnerable to her mildest questions when the scene is critical for old New York. Ellen, in turn, surprises him primarily by dealing simply and naturally with assumptions that seem unduly exciting to him.

But his role as mediator requires more of him. He must simultaneously assume that Ellen has enough merit to be worth salvaging and yet that she represents a danger to old New York. He thinks of her with pity, envy, and suspicion, and this enticing combination, again derived in essence from his official role, sets free his inward yearnings and impulses. Ellen herself needs only touch his knee with her fan to "thrill" his sensibilities. Throughout much of book 1, then, Archer develops new ways of seeing and feeling primarily through the inward implications of being mediator between Ellen and his community. Her occasional words, gestures, and appearances have an impact on Archer so out of proportion to their intrinsic qualities as to suggest that he has not begun to see her as she is, much less to see through her eyes.

Only after Archer has declared his love to her can she begin to show him who she is by trying to make him see what guides her actions and informs her feelings—the moral value she finds in his purely formulary "advice," the richness of a passion that can find its returns inwardly, the honesty to face the full situation in which they find themselves while acknowledging the strong feelings that make such honesty difficult. She develops these attitudes and insights for Archer during the proposal scene, the luncheon in Boston, and the ride in May's carriage, and they represent the substance of her deliberate influence as an agent of rescue. Archer, in turn, learns to admire her for her honesty, her directness, and her seemingly simple way of facing things as they are, without evasion, sentimentality, or undue perturbation; these are qualities he could not see in Ellen during his period of official mediation because they do not correspond to the assumptions of that role. If his role sets free his impulses and perceptions, it is Ellen's more direct function to control and guide his new feelings, to remove the element of perverse delight superimposed on them by his consciousness of acting outside his class limits. That is, by showing him a world in which his newly discovered feelings are as natural, as subject to human scrutiny and judgment, as the habits of old New York, she momentarily saves him from the terrible freedom of a broken law, the anarchic assumption that because one is "wicked," one's feelings and conduct can have no further moral significance. Releasing him from both his conventions and their mere inverse, she allows him to discover states of feeling he could not have anticipated—these are what he saves from their doomed affair.

The delicate inward balance between fulfillment and duty, however, cannot be maintained in New York under the conflicting pressures of social convention and sexual desire. Ellen has transformed both these pressures for Archer by enriching their content. But as his inner life deteriorates, he comes to see in May only the embodiment of restricting habits, and in Ellen only the possibilities of sexual gratification. Thus, when Ellen decides to stay in New York with Mrs. Mingott, Archer feels she has solved their dilemma, now inwardly posed in quite different terms, by yielding to "half-measures" and accepting "the compromise usual in such cases."

In other words, the highly personal problem has become the usual "case," in its passions and issues and strategies, the rules of the game for illicit lovers. Whereas the communal machinery of old New York cannot completely control, cannot even acknowledge, the genuinely individual problem, it is quite adequate to check the usual case. And it does.

The divergence between outer plot and buried fable in *The Age of Innocence*, then, is not represented by the opposition of the community to Archer's love for Ellen. The love triangle itself is, after all, the usual "case" and is as much a part of the overt story as old New York's maneuvers to check it. As long as Archer loves Ellen conventionally, especially in the sexual sense, he has not been released from social determinism but is simply shaking his chains. And here the moral limits of the buried fable are apparent. Sexual pressures become interesting to Edith Wharton by their interplay with other, subtler modes of feeling, some of them involving transfigurations of sexual desire itself. Insofar as the story of inward rescue involves liberation of impulse, this impulse must be brought into a difficult alignment with the rest of the personality; otherwise, it passes out of control and threatens both self and community and must appropriately be quelled by the social order.[6] Only when Archer finds something unique and surprising

[6]This thesis, emerging implicitly in the development of Archer and of several characters in Wharton's other novels (especially *The Fruit of the Tree* and *The Reef*), can easily be reduced to an imperative: the individual must not gain his own satisfaction by flaunting the social order. Even in its harsh and stiffened form, Wharton seems to have believed in this principle. In reviewing Leslie Stephen's *George Eliot* in *Bookman*, 15 (May 1902), 247-51, she emphasizes the relationship between the fictional and the personal problems: "All of George Eliot's noblest characters shrink with a peculiar dread from any personal happiness acquired at the cost of the social organism; yet her own happiness was acquired at such cost" (p. 250). Blake Nevius paraphrases this observation as one of Wharton's major themes: "The individual justification is forced to yield to the larger question of the act's effect on the social structure as a whole" (*Edith Wharton*, p. 112). This dogma, however, presupposes a clear antagonism between the personality and the social order, a struggle in which one or the other must give in, whereas Wharton's fiction presents a more complicated but finally more humane vision. As I try to show in various ways throughout the book, she sees the personality so entangled with the "social organism" that what damages the community inevitably (and perhaps primarily) damages the self as well. (Her argument about George Eliot's fictional career, in fact, demonstrates this point.) There is a danger in reducing analysis and observation to fixed principles, and another of Wharton's comments on George Eliot applies to her own work: "the observer of life is a better writer than the moralist."

in his love for Ellen, and only when he understands his community instead of simply resenting it, do we witness his inward release.

It is the split between what Archer has sacrificed and what he has finally saved that corresponds to the cleavage of overt plot and buried fable. The outer story tells of communal repression and personal failure; the inner story recounts the enrichment of vision and feeling. But this success is strangely muted and delayed, and the very story of its development is essentially linked to the dynamics of the community. It is a story buried within the novel by the outward activities of old New York and of Archer himself, and buried in time by the collapse of the social order on which it depended. Yet Archer's is a moving story, not a quaint period piece, and its power, like that in all of Edith Wharton's best fiction, derives from the interplay of overt plot and buried fable.

What Wharton saw in her social observations was that human behavior, guided by progressively frivolous and arbitrary communal sanctions, was gradually losing its moral significance, and that even when public habits established a coherent basis for judgment, they were so narrow in range as to deny the reality and thus impede the development of essential human possibilities. Her overt plots reflect this estimate of how life is lived. Through the fable of inward release, she shares with her reader a sense of potentiality and anticipation, derived from a larger moral and psychological field, that exactly measures the human cost of what she saw. Of course the overt plot and the buried fable characteristically converge in an act of renunciation, but Wharton brings to that act and to the social circumstances that necessitate it a significance far beyond the register of the social orders she portrays. It is the buried fable that allows her to salvage meaning from what she sees.

Chapter III

Manners in Narrative
The Emergence of Society

THE MOVEMENT OF Edith Wharton's narratives, discussed in the preceding chapter, helps define a society by revealing its most active powers. But this form of definition is incomplete; it tells what a society does, not what it is. Wharton's characters give in too easily in a crisis. They have been conditioned in subtler and more pervasive ways than can be explained by social maneuvers in a contingency. In Wharton's view a society is not a collection of persons but a system of sanctions, customs, and beliefs. It is this system that conditions individuals to submit at critical moments. When Wharton characterizes a social order by depicting its manners, she does not simply tabulate distinct patterns of conduct. Rather she indicates the subtle bonds between them. Her slightest details are both intelligible and weighty because they emerge as parts of an underlying system, and she reveals this system through her techniques for portraying the manners themselves. In this chapter I show, in her three major novels, how Wharton's handling of immediate detail defines a social system and clarifies its significance.

The House of Mirth

During a visit at the Trenors' country estate, Bellomont, Lily Bart awakens one morning to find a note from her hostess asking for some secretarial assistance. This occasional servitude is Lily's obligation for the favor of living in borrowed luxury. As she contemplates her own financial problems, Lily looks about her:

Everything in her surroundings ministered to feelings of ease and amenity. The windows stood open to the sparkling freshness of the September morning, and between the yellow boughs she caught a perspective of hedges and parterres leading by degrees of lessening formality to the free undulations of the park. Her maid had kindled a little fire on the hearth, and it contended cheerfully with the sunlight which slanted across the moss-green carpet and caressed the curved sides of an old marquetry desk. Near the bed stood a table holding her breakfast tray, with its harmonious porcelain and silver, a handful of violets in a slender glass, and the morning paper folded beneath her letters. There was nothing new to Lily in these tokens of a studied luxury; but, though they formed a part of her atmosphere, she never lost her sensitiveness to their charm. Mere display left her with a sense of superior distinction; but she felt an affinity to all the subtler manifestations of wealth. [p. 62]

This scene is more than a realization of the good life from which Lily is soon to fall away. The specific details are enclosed in analytic phrases such as "ease and amenity" and "tokens of a studied luxury." The first sentence of the passage summarizes the deliberate purpose apparent in the setting, and each detail is presented as a calculated effect. The landscape is converted by abstract rendering into a carefully cultivated scene; even the fittings of the breakfast tray are "harmonious." Instead of expanding the sensory qualities of the scene, Wharton abstracts from it the function or design behind the details. This quality of abstraction occurs throughout *The House of Mirth*. When Lily goes for a Sunday stroll, she assumes "a dress somewhat more rustic and summerlike in style than the garment she had first selected" (p. 93). Such phrasing is striking in comparison to the particularities Wharton uses to describe clothing in *The Age of Innocence*. The emphasis in *The House of Mirth* is on the way characters choose their clothing, decoration, and gesture, not on the qualities of what they choose. Manners in *The House of Mirth* are presented in phrases directly accessible to moral judgment instead of sensory response.

One of the most direct ways in which Wharton makes us look for significance in her details is simply by rendering them through moral equivalents. But in this passage it is not only the authorial mind that is interpreting. The discriminations made in the last sentence employ Wharton's moralistic language, but they are Lily's judgments. She recognizes the calculation that has gone into the creation of Bellomont's amenity, and she appreciates it for its subtlety. The calculation implicit in this scene is more than a means for creating comfort and ease; it is designed for social discrimination. The Trenors may be subtle, but they are also snobs. If details in *The House of Mirth* are abstractly rendered in phrases of function, that function is often social exclusion. As Lily descends from class to class in New York society, Wharton distinguishes the manners of each social milieu through abstractions based on a comparison of these manners with those of the Trenor circle. For example, with the Gormers "the difference lay in a hundred shades of aspect and manner, from the pattern of the men's waistcoats to the inflexion of the women's voices. Everything was pitched in a higher key, and there was more of each thing: more noise, more colour, more champagne, more familiarity—but also greater good-nature, less rivalry, and a fresher capacity for enjoyment" (p. 376). The categories open to Lily's judgment here do not represent an absolute moral or aesthetic standard, but simply a means for calculating relative differences in social standing. There is no definable point at which "the subtler manifestations of wealth" become "mere display."

This sense of constant calculation affects Wharton's handling of conversation as well as detail. Even the brightest repartee in the novel is impeded by passages in which she analyzes the choices being made and, in turn, recognized. The characters in this novel scheme as they talk, and they expect the same of others. Personal conversation becomes light verbal play, a contest of skill in which one takes calculated risks that one's real feelings will become involved or, worse yet, apparent. Speaking truthfully is the greatest risk of all, and even honesty emerges as a gambit because of the characters' deliberation about the alternatives.

These tactical qualities underlying manners assume a special potency during public scenes of crisis. The following scene, one of the finest of these, takes place at the Van Alstyne wedding reception. Its critical nature is apparent in the number of distinct narrative pressures it brings to bear on Lily's acts of choice:

There was not the least trace of embarrassment in [Selden's] voice, and as he spoke, leaning slightly against the jamb of the window, and letting his eyes rest on her in the frank enjoyment of her grace, she felt with a faint chill of regret that he had gone back without an effort to the footing on which they had stood before their last talk together. Her vanity was stung by the sight of his unscathed smile. She longed to be to him something more than a piece of sentient prettiness, a passing diversion to his eye and brain; and the longing betrayed itself in her reply.

"Ah," she said, "I envy Gerty that power she has of dressing up with romance all our ugly and prosaic arrangements! I have never recovered my self-respect since you showed me how poor and unimportant my ambitions were."

The words were hardly spoken when she realized their infelicity. It seemed to be her fate to appear at her worst to Selden.

"I thought, on the contrary," he returned lightly, "that I had been the means of proving they were more important to you than anything else."

It was as if the eager current of her being had been checked by a sudden obstacle which drove it back upon itself. She looked at him helplessly, like a hurt or frightened child: this real self of hers, which he had the faculty of drawing out of the depths, was so little accustomed to go alone! ...

"At least you can't think worse things of me than you say!" she exclaimed with a trembling laugh; but before he could answer, the flow of comprehension between them was abruptly stayed by the reappearance of Gus Trenor, who advanced with Mr. Rosedale in his wake.

"Hang it, Lily, I thought you'd given me the slip: Rosedale and I have been hunting all over for you!"

His voice had a note of conjugal familiarity: Miss Bart fancied she detected in Rosedale's eye a twinkling perception of the fact, and the idea turned her dislike of him to repugnance.

She returned his profound bow with a slight nod, made more disdainful by the sense of Selden's surprise that she should number Rosedale among her acquaintances. Trenor had turned away, and his companion continued to stand before Miss Bart, alert and expectant, his lips parted in a smile at whatever she might be about to say, and his very back conscious of the privilege of being seen with her.

It was the moment for tact; for the quick bridging over of gaps; but Selden still leaned against the window, a detached observer of the scene, and under the spell of his observation Lily felt herself powerless to exert her usual arts. The dread of Selden's suspecting that there was any need for her to propitiate such a man as Rosedale checked the trivial phrases of politeness. Rosedale still stood before her in an expectant attitude, and she continued to face him in silence, her glance just level with his polished baldness. The look put the finishing touch to what her silence implied.

He reddened slowly, shifting from one foot to the other, fingered the plump black pearl in his tie, and gave a nervous twist to his moustache; then, running his eye over her, he drew back, and said, with a side-glance at Selden: "Upon my soul, I never saw a more ripping get-up. Is that the last creation of the dress-maker you go to see at the Benedick? If so, I wonder all the other women don't go to her too!"

The words were projected sharply against Lily's silence, and she saw in a flash that her own act had given them their emphasis. In ordinary talk they might have passed unheeded; but following on her prolonged pause they acquired a special meaning. She felt, without looking, that Selden had immediately seized it, and would inevitably connect the allusion with her visit to himself. The consciousness increased her irritation against Rosedale, but also her feeling that now, if ever, was the moment to propitiate him, hateful as it was to do so in Selden's presence.

"How do you know the other women don't go to my dressmaker?" she returned. "You see I'm not afraid to give her address to my friends!"

Her glance and accent so plainly included Rosedale in this privileged circle that his small eyes puckered with gratification, and a knowing smile drew up his moustache.

"By Jove, you needn't be!" he declared. "You could give 'em the whole outfit and win at a canter!"

"Ah, that's nice of you; and it would be nicer still if you would carry me off to a quiet corner, and get me a glass of lemonade or some innocent drink before we all have to rush for the train." [pp. 151-55]

The irony of Lily's relationship with Selden is that although he is the one person who can draw out her real self, he can never trust her or meet her openness seriously. Wharton's narrative analysis leaves no question about the kind of "footing" Lily wishes to assume with Selden, especially after their talk about "the republic of the spirit," but her "longing" is expressed too openly in her words to him, and he replies in a tone calculated to bring their relationship back to light repartee. For all Selden's criticism of his society, he cannot avoid talking within its framework. At the moment when Lily most obviously wants support in expressing feelings that have no place in a calculating society, Selden's banter turns out to be the very embodiment of that society's artificial tone. Only when her plight appeals indirectly to his vanity does he prepare to take her more seriously.

If polite conversation is a test of skill in shifting tone, Wharton's means for presenting gesture and inflection emphasize the changes in assumed relationships. Trenor's voice has "a note of conjugal familiarity"; Rosedale's eye shows a "twinkling perception of the fact"; Lily's slight nod is "disdainful"; and her "glance and accent . . . plainly included Rosedale in this privileged circle." These manners, like the details discussed earlier, are conveyed in generalized language, emphasizing their function, and that function is to assume a deliberate social relationship—in simplest terms, acceptance or exclusion. The manners of Simon Rosedale, who has yet to learn the ways of the Trenor circle, are subject to a different notation; when Wharton directly describes his low bow, his fingering of the black pearl, and his coarse physical appraisal of Lily, she implies that the parvenu's behavior is obviously subject to scorn, even without narrative analysis, and she unfortunately extends this implied communion with her reader by appealing to the "polite" anti-Semitism of her own and Lily's class. But such covert appeals to "taste" by direct observation of detail are relatively rare in *The House of Mirth;* Wharton more characteristically presents manners through abstracting phrases like "a gesture of appropriation" or "a gesture in which dismissal was shorn of its rigor."

Her procedure in the reception scene suggests more, however, than assumed social relationships. She asks us to believe that shifts in tone and taste are moral changes. When Rosedale seems to note Trenor's meaning, the idea turns Lily's "dislike of him to repugnance," and the "dread of Selden's suspecting that there was any need for her to propitiate such a man as Rosedale checked the trivial phrases of politeness." The effect of such weighty phrasing is to turn light verbal play into a morally earnest duel, in which the test of skill is how much Lily must sacrifice to extricate herself. In this instance, as in several others, Lily uses her social and physical desirability as an evasive promise veiled behind her polite phrasing. But Wharton has so heightened our expectations by phrases such as "it was the moment for tact" and "now, if ever, was the moment to propitiate him" that we know Lily's "usual arts" will not allow her a complete moral recovery. She can maintain social poise, but only at the cost of establishing an immediately unpleasant intimacy as well as implying future favors for her antagonist.

And here we face the problem of relating manners to morals: why should a pretty girl's introduction to a bounder at a party constitute a grave moral crisis? The answer is implied by Wharton's presentation of manners. We are confronted with a society in which gestures, talk, and decorative art are calculated to represent discrimination and exclusion. Appearances hurt, as is evident in the power of Rosedale's innuendo about the Benedick. In spite of such deliberation about manners, however, they represent neither a fixed social order nor an absolute standard of judgment. Consequently, manners are only the social surface of a struggle between various kinds of power—reputation, sexuality or physical beauty, family background and race, and, most important, money. In the reception scene Lily is acting under intense pressure from several directions: her fastidiousness and her social prejudice make her recoil from Rosedale; her real self remains conscious of Selden's detached judgment; her need for the money Trenor has given her keeps her from evading Rosedale; and, more generally, she wants to maintain her place in the only society she knows. It is these pressures, in large part determined by her own background, that give others conspicuous power over Lily and complicate her social behavior with morally serious issues and ambiguities.

On the one hand, then, social relations in this novel emerge as a game. The individual players implicate themselves in this game not only by deliberating about their own moves but by looking for and recognizing the gambits of others. They know the rules, and the more skillfully they play, the more they habituate themselves to the reality circumscribed by the game itself. On the other hand, the stakes vary from player to player; for some, including Lily, the game can be deadly serious. Thus, while Wharton accentuates the artificiality of the game by repeated contrasts between the natural and the calculated, she shows that the artifice itself cannot be lightly dismissed. As we yearn for the spontaneous, we must examine the contrived. And she presents this game-oriented society through a rhetoric of heavy moral judgment and discrimination. Between the demands created and the conditions projected in *The House of Mirth,* no compromise is possible.

The Custom of the Country

The world that confronts us in *The Custom of the Country* bears close historical connections with that in *The House of Mirth,* but Wharton's handling of manners in the later novel suggests a new set of narrative interests. Here are two passages describing the Spragg accommodations at a West Side hotel in New York:

Mrs. Spragg and her visitor were enthroned in two heavy gilt armchairs in one of the private drawing-rooms of the Hotel Stentorian. The Spragg rooms were known as one of the Looey suites, and the drawing-room walls, above their wainscoting of highly-varnished mahogany, were hung with salmon-pink damask and adorned with oval portraits of Marie Antoinette and the Princess de Lamballe. In the centre of the florid carpet a gilt table with a top of Mexican onyx sustained a palm in a gilt basket tied with a pink bow. But for this ornament, and a copy of "The Hound of the Baskervilles" which lay beside it, the room showed no traces of human use, and Mrs. Spragg herself wore as complete an air of detachment as if she had been a wax figure in a show-window. Her attire was fashionable enough to justify such a post, and her pale soft-cheeked face, with puffy eyelids and drooping mouth, suggested a partially-melted wax figure which had run to double-chin. [p. 4]

[Undine] came dawdling into the sodden splendour of the Stentorian breakfast-room. . . .

Mr. Spragg, having finished the last course of his heterogeneous meal, was adjusting his gold eye-glasses for a glance at the paper when Undine trailed down the sumptuous stuffy room, where coffee-fumes hung perpetually under the emblazoned ceiling and the spongy carpet might have absorbed a year's crumbs without a sweeping.

About them sat other pallid families, richly dressed, and silently eating their way through a bill-of-fare which seemed to have ransacked the globe for gastronomic incompatibilities; and in the middle of the room a knot of equally pallid waiters, engaged in languid conversation, turned their backs by common consent on the persons they were supposed to serve. . . . Mrs. Spragg [pushed] aside the bananas and cream with which she had been trying to tempt an appetite too languid for fried liver or crab mayonnaise. [pp. 40-41]

Clearly we are in a comic world, but we will miss its significance if we only respond to it lightly. These families, newly arrived in New York with their Midwest money, are in grim earnest about seeking social preferment. One of the apparent differences in Wharton's control of manners here is that she depends less on functional abstractions than on selection of detail. Her method is related to her handling of Rosedale with Lily; she implies a communion of taste with her reader, assuming that it is obviously ridiculous to mix *The Hound of the Baskervilles* and a portrait of Marie Antoinette. Similarly, she depends on our agreeing that the ornamentation of the room has accumulated to the point of absurdity. If we were to ask the narrator for her standards of judgment here, she would be thrown back on something like "good taste." In other words, the narrative voice in *The Custom of the Country* betrays more snobbery than that of *The House of Mirth*. The moralistic phrasing of the earlier book is replaced by adjectives and lofty phrases charged with social scorn. Whereas "studied luxury" and "harmonious porcelain and silver" represent details by their moral equivalents, "sodden splendour" and "gastronomic incompatibilities" sum up a series of specific details and dismiss them sharply.

The details here present a curious ambivalence in comparison to those of *The House of Mirth:* they are at once more concrete and less substantial. The Stentorian is more immediately accessible to the senses than Bellomont, but the specific details clash with each other, and they reflect no settled convictions, even about social discrimination. Mrs. Spragg bears no relationship to her surroundings, and they certainly do not minister to her comfort. Details are selected to suggest mutual incompatibility, shifting taste, and gaudiness.

What are the implications of these specific but incongruous details? They certainly do not reveal coherent choice by the characters. Our first encounter with domestic life in *The Custom of the Country* is in a hotel. By its very nature, such a setting cannot reflect the ideals of its inhabitants. Wharton has chosen this setting because she is concerned with a state of affairs characteristic of New York society as it lost its connection with the standards of its mercantile aristocracy. Hotels become representative of a new way of life. Though less sophisticated, the Stentorian can be classed with the Nouveau Luxe in Paris, the social center for American travelers in Europe. The society passing through the Nouveau Luxe is composed of conspicuously wealthy Americans, degenerate European aristocrats, counterfeit Bohemians, and parasites. It represents "what unbounded material power had devised for the delusion of its leisure: a phantom 'society,' with all the rules, smirks, gestures of its model, but evoked out of promiscuity and incoherence while the other had been the product of continuity and choice" (p. 273). The Nouveau Luxe reflects the uncertain desires associated with a general drifting of society. The people assembled there are rootless. They may be more brilliant and beguiling than the Spraggs at the Stentorian, but they are a part of the same phenomenon. The Spraggs have cut themselves off from their real past in Apex, and they cannot come to terms with what they find in New York. Even their physical appearances are losing their outlines. Mrs. Spragg does not want French portraits and a gilt table any more than she wants crab mayonnaise for breakfast. What she wants is happiness for her daughter, and she lets her immediate desires be dictated by Undine's prescriptions.

But how does Undine decide what she wants and how she will behave? As the novel opens, she is invited to dinner by Ralph

Marvell's sister, Mrs. Fairford. Only after Mrs. Heeny, the "society" masseuse, pronounces the Marvells stylish, does Undine consider the note seriously.

"It *is* written to mother—Mrs. Abner E. Spragg—I never saw anything so funny! 'Will you *allow* your daughter to dine with me?' Allow! Is Mrs. Fairford peculiar?"

"No—you are," said Mrs. Heeny bluntly. "Don't you know it's the thing in the best society to pretend that girls can't do anything without their mothers' permission? You just remember that, Undine. You mustn't accept invitations from gentlemen without you say you've got to ask your mother first." [p. 9]

Undine prepares to write a note of acceptance for her mother, but she must make several decisions.

She had read in the "Boudoir Chat" of one of the Sunday papers that the smartest women were using the new pigeon-blood notepaper with white ink; and rather against her mother's advice she had ordered a large supply, with her monogram in silver. It was a disappointment, therefore, to find that Mrs. Fairford wrote on the old-fashioned white sheet, without even a monogram—simply her address and telephone number. It gave Undine rather a poor opinion of Mrs. Fairford's social standing, and for a moment she thought with considerable satisfaction of answering the note on her pigeon-blood paper. Then she remembered Mrs. Heeny's emphatic commendation of Mrs. Fairford, and her pen wavered. What if white paper were really newer than pigeon-blood? It might be more stylish, anyhow. Well, she didn't care if Mrs. Fairford didn't like red paper—*she* did! And she wasn't going to truckle to any woman who lived in a small house down beyond Park Avenue. . . .

Undine was fiercely independent and yet passionately imitative. She wanted to surprise every one by her dash and originality, but she could not help modelling herself on the last person she met, and the confusion of ideals thus produced caused her much perturbation when she had to choose between two courses. She hesitated a moment longer, and then took from the drawer a plain sheet with the hotel address. . . . [After writing the note,] she resolutely formed the signature: "Sincerely, Mrs. Abner E. Spragg." Then uncertainty overcame her, and she re-wrote her note and copied Mrs. Fairford's formula: "Yours sincerely, Leota B. Spragg." But this struck her as an odd juxtaposition of formality and freedom, and she made a third attempt: "Yours with love, Leota B. Spragg." This, however, seemed excessive, as the ladies had never met; and after several other experiments she finally decided on a compromise, and ended the note: "Yours sincerely, Mrs. Leota B. Spragg." That might be conventional, Undine reflected, but it was certainly correct. [pp. 18-20]

This passage suggests why the narrative voice here tends toward snobbery: Wharton has brought her point of view in considerably closer to the perceptions and thoughts of her central characters. We are encouraged to measure social standing and taste by surface details because Undine herself is so deeply concerned with what is "smart," "new," and "stylish." By sharing Undine's deliberation over the signature, we are forced into a realm of judgment in which it seems pertinent to notice that her final choice is not "certainly correct." This is the pattern of much of the book's satire. But at the same time, Undine's perspective emphasizes the insecurity of social behavior. It simply ought not to be so difficult to write a note. Undine wastes her energy and frustrates herself making trivial choices that could be expedited by settled conventions. By a series of such seemingly petty uncertainties, Wharton reinforces one value of accepted manners—they can facilitate human relations. Once Undine abandons the conventions of Apex, she must be painstakingly instructed about what is "smart" and what is "the thing." And Mrs. Heeny's advice suggests what happens to manners in such instruction. They become purely formulary, losing all reference to deeper values or to human relations. One merely "pretends."

With no stable institutions to determine her manners, Undine must seek models to imitate. Like the undulating water from which her name is taken, she is a shapeshifter. Her liking for pigeon-blood notepaper has been determined by the "Boudoir Chat," a fact she overlooks in asserting her mental independence from Mrs. Fairford. But as Mrs. Fairford has been declared stylish, Undine copies her, with some compromises. There is no shortage of models for Undine; there are too many and they disagree. Her life is a series of shifts from a "Boudoir Chat" to a Mrs. Fairford. "Once more all the accepted values were reversed. . . . To know that others were indifferent to what she had thought important was to cheapen all present pleasure and turn the whole force of her desires in a new direction" (p. 286).

In his fine study *Deceit, Desire and the Novel*, René Girard describes a phenomenon that he calls "triangular desire."[1] Between

---

[1] René Girard, *Deceit, Desire and the Novel*, trans. Yvonne Freccero (Baltimore, 1965).

a subject and an object he thinks he desires, stands a mediator. The subject has modeled himself on the mediator, who has in turn determined the object of desire. Triangular desire transfigures the object by shedding on it a brilliance of illusory abstractions. The mediator's suggestion replaces the subject's own impression, and the mediator becomes a kind of divinity whose ritualistic gestures imply that he knows the secret of the good life. This phenomenon presents serious problems when the mediator is one's neighbor in a world where social differences are no longer sharply defined, for the mediator then competes with the subject for the same desired object, and the emotions of rivalry, envy, and jealousy become dominant.

Undine Spragg moves in such a world. She is pathetically dependent on others in finding out what she wants and how she should act, but her shifting society places her so close to her mediators that she is repeatedly disillusioned and thus constantly tempted to change models. She marries Ralph Marvell because New York society desires his presence at dinner parties, and her "love" increases when she learns that Clare Van Degen has loved him for years; "Undine always liked to know that what belonged to her was coveted by others" (p. 226). Because her desires need conspicuous approval, she is content only in public. When forced to fall back on her own taste, judgment, or ideas, as in answering Mrs. Fairford's note, Undine faces inner vacancy.

The surface of Undine's life, like the surface of the overall social world in this novel, appears in perpetual change. When Undine and Elmer Moffatt finally marry and establish themselves in a private *hôtel* in Paris, furnished in costly magnificence, Wharton presents their triumph as barren. In a scene significantly composed of things, she summarizes the meaning of imitative desire and reveals the underlying horror of the social scene she has been projecting. She describes the *hôtel* through the eyes of Undine's nine-year-old son, who has come to see his mother on holiday, and his perfectly natural desires interpret the scene. While waiting for Undine, he eats alone in the immense marble dining room and wanders from room to room, afraid to touch the objects that rouse his curiosity, afraid even to sit down on the gold armchairs in the drawing room or the brocade chairs in his own room. He tries to look at one of Moffatt's books, but they are locked behind gilt trellising—they are too valuable to be read. Looking for company or for something to do, he encounters objects, and the most conspicuous thing about them is their evident costliness. He feels like a stranger in his mother's home. Here is a setting in which form simply denies function. Real human needs are thwarted by the meretricious desire to be "in it." Like Undine herself, the *hôtel* is arresting to the eye but not to be touched.

The presentation of manners in *The Custom of the Country* conveys strong feelings of uncertainty and discomfort. Manners have become detached from any recognizable meaning or function. Desire and behavior are imitated without purpose or understanding, and the choice of models is virtually arbitrary. Consequently, the surface of society is set in an aimless drift, and the only details that are recognizable to characters like Undine are those that are conspicuous for their size, brightness, noise, motion, or expense. By cutting themselves off from their own past and from any stable institutions, such characters lose their ability to understand human experience. Their manners become arbitrary gestures, meaningless at best and possibly harmful. The caustic and impatient narrative voice reflects Wharton's frustration with a society becoming incomprehensible.

Whereas the air of calculation in *The House of Mirth* makes the reader look in vain for honesty and openness, the sense of unsubstantiality and aimless motion in *The Custom of the Country* implies a different set of normative desires. Here we look for examples of integrity, continuity, restfulness, for manners that reflect a character's past and his ideals, for furnishings that conduce to real human activities. And Ralph Marvell, who shares Wharton's values, shows by his own frustration that such ideals are doomed. After he has seen what Undine is, he retreats from her world of garish brilliance and personal indifference to Clare Van Degen's "shady drawing-room." Here he finds "luxurious silences," a "soberer background," "the final touch of well-being." Gesture and setting satisfy his needs, and as another inheritor of the Dagonet traditions, Ralph's cousin can give him understanding and peace. But as he recognizes, "Clare's taste was as capricious as her moods, and the rest of the house was not in harmony with this room" (p. 319). She has helped old New York make its social transition by marrying the wealthy, unscrupulous Peter Van Degen.

In the midst of a description of the room in which Clare receives
Ralph, a setting that reflects the social amenities of Washington
Square, Wharton inserts a reference to her other drawing room,
the one representing the gaudier tastes of Upper Fifth Avenue.
Ralph must deliberate about which is the "real" Clare, and the
question is by no means settled, for she will soon receive him in
the gilt room. Even the social traditions of Washington Square
offer no firm footing; Clare represents old New York's gradual
accommodation to new wealth, strident manners, and a relaxed
moral tone. The ground is shifting under Ralph Marvell's feet.
Everything is, or threatens to become, unreal.

The Age of Innocence

In her most complex and successful study of manners, Wharton
analyzes the weaknesses in the amenable social traditions of old
New York that caused them to fail sensitive characters like Ralph
Marvell and Newland Archer and finally to collapse themselves.
But she also presents here a peculiar communal strength. Although
old New York was far from her ideal society, its manners were
still connected with real human activities. The details in *The Age of
Innocence* are more immediate than those in *The House of Mirth*
and more substantial than those in *The Custom of the Country*
because the manners of old New York represent for her a coherent
attitude toward life. By the time she wrote this novel, however,
old New York had disappeared, and her historical distance also
contributes to the change in her handling of manners. When she
writes of the contemporaneous, she presents manners through con-
trolling abstractions if she does not entirely disapprove of them;
specificity of detail serves satiric purposes. Here her distance allows
her to criticize and to admire at the same time, and the immediacy
arises from nostalgia. She is evoking a lost way of life.

To see how her criticism blends with her nearly archaeological
zeal, one could look at almost any descriptive passage early in the
book, such as the section of chapter 3 devoted to the Beaufort
house on the night of the annual ball. One is struck by the analytical cast of the observations, the constant comparison and
evaluation. The Beauforts are "among the first" in New York to

own the awning and carpet for the ball instead of renting them, and they "inaugurate" the custom of having the ladies remove their cloaks in the hall. In the first instance, such analysis places the scene historically and emphasizes the immersion of old New York in social change. Wharton does not simply describe the Beauforts' house and their way of giving a ball; she stresses the changes they are making. Manners here tend to indicate historical development more than social position. They are not being imitated by outsiders so much as they are undergoing innovation, prodded along by semioutsiders like Beaufort and eccentric insiders like Mrs. Mingott. Beaufort boldly plans his house in such a way that old New Yorkers can get to the ballroom more comfortably and impressively than at other houses, "seeing from afar the many-candled lustres reflected in the polished parquetry, and beyond that the depths of a conservatory where camellias and tree-ferns arched their costly foliage over seats of black and gold bamboo." As they begin to feel the effects of new money, they are even proud of Beaufort. That he can give a better ball than they are accustomed to, obscurely makes up for his "audacity" in hanging Bouguereau's nude in his drawing room. His scandalous bank failure later in the book will profoundly shock old New York because his entertainments have implicated traditional society in the world of financial manipulation.

But the historical analysis underlying the very conception of the scene emerges indirectly, for Wharton has incorporated the angle of vision within the perceptions of what might be described as a communal intelligence. Specifically, we see over Newland Archer's shoulder, but his attitudes in these early chapters so entirely reflect old New York that we view the ball, in effect, as New Yorkers do. This accounts, in part, for the immediate, vivid, and inviting details: "the light of the wax candles fell on revolving tulle skirts, on girlish heads wreathed with modest blossoms, on the dashing aigrettes and ornaments of the young married women's *coiffures,* and on the glitter of highly glazed shirt-fronts and fresh glacé gloves." The scene is accessible to the senses, and it is animated by the darting movement of a participant's eye. But the communal point of view also represents a cast of thought. It is the immediate source of the analytic tendencies in the passage. It is not Wharton but old New York that compares this ball to the Chiverses' and notes Beaufort's "audacity" and "fatuities" (his footmen wear silk stockings). The profound relation of manners to perceptions appears in the communal reaction to subtle changes in behavior.

We are confronted with a society that concentrates on the foreground of experience, that is alive to particular manners as evidence, not of acceptance or exclusion, but of propriety or disintegration. The informing quality of old New York is the complex system of interpretation accompanying its manners, and the subtle, discriminating cast of mind shared by old New Yorkers indicates both the strength and the weakness of this system. The refined interpretation of behavior is based on an acute sense of "good form." Throughout the novel particular observations are filtered through a screen of custom; we are constantly reminded of the way things have always been done. Archer arrives at the ball late, "as became a young man of his position," and we learn in a characteristic parenthesis that the "young bloods" usually go to the club after the opera. The rigidity of these customs suggests a rough equivalence in the various ways of "going too far"—there seems to be no way of distinguishing the bad form of a young man coming on time to a ball and that of the Mingotts bringing a "disgraced" countess. The system thus encourages disproportionate responses— Archer cannot simply defend the Countess Olenska, he must "champion" her. His phrasing of his determination during the ball to "see the thing through" reveals a standardized response in which lapses from good manners appear in moral formulas.

The weaknesses of this system are most evident when the New Yorker encounters new ways of behaving, as Archer does in chapter 9 when he first visits Ellen Olenska's house in the "Bohemian" quarter. By having Ellen herself out when Archer arrives, Wharton contrives a scene in which the young man can respond to the setting while he waits; she then illustrates the effects of that setting on his personal relationship with Ellen. The curious thing about Archer's view of her room is that he cannot see much. He spots a few details—some slender tables, a Greek bronze, a stretch of red damask—and his mind darts away. Most of the particularities of interior decoration in his mind do not involve Ellen's house at all but a projection of the house in East Thirty-ninth Street where he and May will live. He cannot come to terms with the unforeseen style of Ellen Olenska except by referring back to the interiors he has learned to see. As in the description of the Beaufort ball, the analysis here sets the scene historically and emphasizes signs of change. Young architects are striking out from the uniformity of New York's brownstone, and the freer spirits who have read Charles Eastlake's *Hints on Household Taste* (first published in America in 1872) have learned how to rebel against the ornamental excrescences of the Victorian interior. Thus Archer assumes that May will simply carry on her parents' style—"purple satin and yellow tuftings . . . sham Buhl tables and gilt vitrines"—whereas he will break away from the conventional by arranging his library as he pleases, "which would be, of course, with 'sincere' Eastlake furniture, and the plain new bookcases without glass doors." His smug sense of originality blinds him to the fact that the lines of his rebellion have already been laid down. The conventions themselves are changing, and, like New Yorkers attending Beaufort's ball, Archer is simply moving with the times.

But how does his mental excursion into New York's interior decorating help him place Ellen's house? Her style does not fit, and Archer's perceptions are so bound up in the conventional that he cannot see her drawing room specifically. Instead he feels "the sense of adventure"; he confronts the scene abstractly ("the way the chairs and tables were grouped") and stylizes its effect— "something intimate, 'foreign,' subtly suggestive of old romantic scenes and sentiments." The New Yorker's intense concentration on the surface of life makes him acute in recognizing deviations from the customary—"only two Jacqueminot roses (of which nobody ever bought less than a dozen)," "perfume that was not what one put on handkerchiefs"—but such scrutiny also places undue emphasis on the mere fact of deviation. The unusual becomes the "foreign," and because of New York's blending of manners and morals, the foreign is associated with the suggestive and the romantic. Instead of assessing the arrangement of a room, Archer finds himself confronting something alien, immoral, and extraordinarily enticing.

With such a cast of thought, more is at stake than aesthetic simplification or imprecision. Archer is virtually seduced by a room, and once Ellen herself returns, his behavior is confused by his previous excitement. He means to warn her about being seen with Beaufort, "but he was being too deeply drawn into the

atmosphere of the room, which was her atmosphere, and to give
advice of that sort would have been like telling some one who was
bargaining for attar-of-roses in Samarkand that one should always
be provided with arctics for a New York winter" (pp. 73-74). In
this bewildering milieu, his conventional moralizing can find no
hold. Moreover, once the New Yorker has noted a divergence from
accepted forms, he has no way to measure degrees of foreignness.
If perfume is not like what one puts on a handkerchief, it suggests
"a far-off bazaar." The unusual quickly extends into the most
exotic, and Archer finally feels as far from New York as Samarkand. This vulnerability to the unforeseen is the most obvious
weakness of old New York's manners. Having stepped outside his
conventions, Archer can no more assess his personal ties with Ellen
than he can account for the decoration of her room. It seems as if
he must either disregard what his system cannot explain or discard
the system itself as irrelevant to his experience.

But if Archer's social habits schematize Ellen's nature, the
complexities of his own system are also obscured in the disorient-
ing context of his experience with the "foreign." It is on its home
ground that Wharton can indicate the subtler expense and the
finer compensation of old New York's system, as she does during
chapter 30 in a scene between Archer and May. They dine alone
and spend the evening in the library, a characteristic context in
which to observe the domestic side of New York's manners. But
this is also a special evening, for Ellen has returned to New York,
and Archer, delegated to meet her at the station that afternoon,
found himself so agitated by his feelings for her that he walked
home, forgetting his promise to meet May at Mrs. Mingott's house.
There is thus considerable strain between husband and wife in the
scene, however much it may be concealed.

The strain is most apparent as Archer feels it, for we see from
his perspective. The imagery, theme, and selection of detail here
emphasize monotony and oppressiveness, and one does not need
Archer's experience with the "foreign" to suffer from such entrapment. All one needs is inward cravings; that old New York cannot
acknowledge these represents one of its major failings. While the
heaviness of the detail reflects Archer's immediate feelings—May's
workbasket under his green-shaded student lamp, her wedding ring
moving painstakingly above her embroidery—the effect of the

details also arises from accumulation. Throughout the novel Wharton has been circumstantially describing the interiors of old New York, the enclosures of its domestic life. It is not surprising in such a context that Archer needs to open the library window, to get "the sense of other lives outside his own" and clear his head. But even so simple and symbolic a gesture is enmeshed in more decorative detail: "He had insisted that the library curtains should draw backward and forward on a rod, so that they might be closed in the evening, instead of remaining nailed to a gilt cornice, and immovably looped up over layers of lace, as in the drawing-room."

Wharton has been accumulating more than details, however. By this point she has presented so many interpretations of the customary that old New York's manners appear as a complete system, the full weight of which can be felt in each detail. May has on the tightly laced dinner dress exacted by "the Mingott ceremonial"; her hair has its "usual accumulated coils"; her face, "its usual tenderness"; and the dinner talk, "its usual limited circle." While Archer reads after dinner, she embroiders a cushion for him because wives embroider cushions for their husbands, and "this last link of her devotion" completes a chain binding Archer to her and both of them to the entire social order. Thus Archer feels her presence not simply as May but as the incarnation of a system. She is, for Archer, so overwhelmingly *there*, in his library, at his table, under his student lamp, "laboriously stabbing the canvas," that he focuses his discontent on her and momentarily wishes her dead.

Although Archer's feelings are comprehensible under the circumstances, his behavior and motives in the scene are not attractive, and it is in revealing his cruelty to May that Wharton explores the other potentialities of old New York. Archer's own interpretations of May's conduct here suggest the immense significance of silences; that she makes no allusion to Ellen during dinner strikes him as "vaguely ominous." This mode of communication is rooted in communal manners. Throughout the novel New Yorkers talk by glances and "faint implications." "In reality they all lived in a kind of hieroglyphic world, where the real thing was never said or done or even thought, but only represented by a set of arbitrary signs" (p. 42). These hieroglyphics make the social surface dense and significant, and the complex system of inter-

pretation necessitated by them defines the peculiar strength of old
New York. It demands astute perception, subtle analysis, and
careful attention to a social code and to another person. Such
habits obviously discourage outright selfishness and insensibility.
No matter how limited the range of moral content may be in New
York, at least its forms enrich the moral life. And Wharton elucidates these forms so thoroughly that one is drawn into the same
system of interpretation; from this perspective one judges Archer
in the scene.

Ironically, the personal cost of Archer's rebellion is estimated
within the potentialities of the very system he finds so stifling. He
is so absorbed with his own feelings that he ignores the set of signs
between himself and May. He forgets that he can send as well as
receive hieroglyphic messages, that his own silence about Ellen
tells more disturbing things than May's. When they go to the
library he takes down a volume of Michelet: "He had taken to
history in the evenings since May had shown a tendency to ask
him to read aloud whenever she saw him with a volume of poetry."
Again May seems to discern his meaning here, for only after
"seeing that he had chosen history," does she fetch that oppressive
embroidery. And his sense of her as a responsibility, as the embodiment of the oppressive system, blinds him as well to the
personal messages she is sending. He assumes with dismay as he
glances at her in the library, that he will always know what goes on
behind her "clear brow," that she will never surprise him "by an
unexpected mood, by a new idea, a weakness, a cruelty, or an
emotion." But this is to deny his own astuteness within the system,
for only a week earlier he constructed a whole paragraph in "code"
from one of May's statements, attributing to her an awareness of
his feelings about Ellen. May's "wan and almost faded face" at
dinner, her "strained laugh" at his condescending pity in the
library, her hesitation before changing the artificially light tone
and telling him "I shall never worry if you're happy"—all these
ought, against such a background, to be telling signs, but for
Archer they are mere appearances. The subjects of Ellen's arrival,
his trip back from the station with her, and his neglect of his
promise to meet May would no doubt have been as painful to her
at dinner as to himself.

Her "clear brow," then, is not the appalling sign of innocence that Archer reads, but the indication of her self-control. And such control illustrates the other major strength of old New York's manners: they sustain personal dignity while providing a delicate measure of one's feelings and sacrifices. May's ceremonial appearance at dinner, despite her suffering and suspicion, combines with her resolute effort to do her domestic duty even though "she was not a clever needle-woman," to elevate and to enlarge her character. Near the end of the novel Archer reflects on his marriage to May: "Their long years together had shown him that it did not so much matter if marriage was a dull duty, as long as it kept the dignity of a duty: lapsing from that, it became a mere battle of ugly appetites" (p. 350). The scene in the library is far from a battle of ugly appetites.

Thus, while Wharton clearly and firmly indicts old New York for its evasiveness, its vulnerability, and its narrowness, she indicates the complexity of the social order by showing how its virtues arise from its very defects. If the New Yorker is overly excited by the "foreign," he also finds in it more joy and subtle possibility than would be perceptible from a less provincial perspective. The richness of Ellen Olenska emerges largely from the way in which she is seen. If the "hieroglyphic world" encourages misunderstanding and evasion, it also enforces delicacy of perception. The complex interlocking of manners and their interpretation makes daily life oppressive; yet at the same time it habituates the mind to careful, serious analysis. And the very narrowness and rigidity of the system sustain at least one kind of personal dignity; no one in *The Age of Innocence* is quite so pathetic, foolish, or bewildered as most of the characters Wharton presents as the products of New York's later days.

The qualities Edith Wharton saw in old New York provided her with the materials not only to write one of the purest novels of manners in American fiction but to probe the very possibilities of human experience as predicated on manners. She shows in *The Age of Innocence* how a social order can create a meaningful area of human life. In her earlier novels she demonstrates the importance of manners primarily in a negative fashion, by their powers of impairing the individual life or by their inadequacy to human needs; the significance of manners lies in their capacity to impinge on values determined within another framework entirely, on personal development, for instance, or honesty or coherence. Old New York, on the other hand, generates meaning and value positively: it creates serious issues of conduct; it encourages subtle modes of understanding; and it develops in its products qualities of character that cannot be laughed away, stuffy as they may seem. When its values aré wrong or arbitrarily narrow, at least they are intelligibly so; and the coherence of its habits and its means of interpreting them provides a stable configuration of values against which an individual's divergence and growth can be estimated with fine clarity. Old New York is obviously not a satisfactory social order, but it *is* a social order.

Chapter IV

Characterization
Manners and Psychology

THE NOVEL OF manners often abounds with well-drawn and vivid characters. By observing class differences and particularities of behavior, the novelist can locate details that solidify and define the individual. Furthermore, the social background against which a character is defined gives significance to his actions and substantiates the issues of his moral conduct. But in Edith Wharton's fiction the very richness of social analysis weakens the characterization. She conceives her characters within a framework of inquiry that limits the range of their imagined humanity. As a novelist deeply engaged with the problems of social organization, she initially visualizes her characters as representatives of certain social phenomena—institutions, classes, historical movements—and she develops them not by stressing their individuality but by elaborating the working powers of the phenomena they represent. She follows her own suggestion in *The Writing of Fiction* that one can eliminate unnecessary characters from the novel of manners by making each figure typify a whole section of the social background. And her concern for the effects of manners on the individual soul leads her to conceive her major figures as victims of social convention.

But the moral commitments that play against Wharton's social observations have a counterpart in her theories about the drawing of character. Rather than subscribe to rigid formulas of environmental or psychological determinism, she sees human life as conducted on reasonably coherent and selective lines. She treats her major characters as if they were responsible beings, and she sees her own craft as the careful elucidation of this responsibility. Three years before her death Wharton wrote a critique of contemporary fiction that reflects, even in the rigidity of her later conservatism, some of the basic commitments of her characterization. In the "slice of life," the "stream of consciousness," and fiction about "the man with the dinner pail," she found a common flaw—random selection of material without guiding convictions:

It is obviously much easier to depict rudimentary characters, moved from the cradle to the grave by the same unchanging handful of instincts and prejudices, than to follow the actions of persons in whom education and opportunity have developed a more complex psychology. For the same reason it is easier to note the confused drift of subconscious sensation than to single out the conscious thoughts and deliberate actions which are the key to character, and to the author's reason for depicting that character.[1]

This comment suggests that Wharton thought of characterization in Aristotelian terms: character is portrayed in serious actions through moral choices. In her earlier fiction she emphasizes the possibility of such choices by her own moral analyses, but in books like *The Custom of the Country* and *The Age of Innocence* she records actions and thought processes in which deliberation often plays a smaller part than social convention. For Ralph Marvell and Newland Archer, character is defined less by deliberate moral action than by subsequent reflection. The moral lives of her central characters emerge only *after* they have muddled their way through a crisis, guided by instinct, emotion, and convention. When forced to make a moral recovery, they discover themselves by the patient scrutiny of their previous experience. But they do make moral recoveries, and in the discrepancy between the "confused drift" of their sentiments or habitudes and the "conscious thoughts" that mark their recoveries, one sees Wharton's effort to single out the key to character from all those aspects of the self that are common, instinctive, or socially decreed.

In distinguishing "rudimentary characters" from those with "education and opportunity," however, Wharton unfortunately echoes a social era that could condemn Dickens for never having drawn "a gentleman." The distinction rests, of course, on the intricacy and social prestige of a character's class, but when Wharton sees education and opportunity as developing "a more complex psychology," she locates the line of interest that was to vivify her few substantial major characters—the relationship between a set of manners and the devious turnings of the individual psyche. In order

---

[1]Edith Wharton, "Tendencies in Modern Fiction," *Saturday Review of Literature*, 10 (27 Jan. 1934), 434.

to understand these individualizing qualities, one must begin with the social representativeness that figured as the basic component of her characterization.

The Institutional Self

In the work of a novelist primarily interested in the meaning and effect of society, it is natural that minor and major characters alike should be defined as products of particular social practices. Wharton does not impose a deterministic framework after imagining her characters as free and self-defined; she conceives them as the results or representatives of a social system. The differences between Ralph Marvell and Raymond de Chelles in their capacities to cope with Undine Spragg, for instance, are largely attributed to the institutions of old New York and those of France. The French family and its far-reaching extensions, together with the Roman Catholic Church, provide a network of traditional attitudes and obligations that subordinate the self to a powerful and indivisible whole. Raymond's personal force to resist Undine, even when he still loves her, arises from the stability and certainty of purpose instilled by this larger network, which has only a much-diminished counterpart in Ralph's affiliations with Washington Square.

Undine herself is more centrally defined as "a monstrously perfect result" of the system which provides the title *The Custom of the Country* and which produces several of Wharton's other women as well, such as Bessie Amherst in *The Fruit of the Tree*. This system in Wharton's analysis derives from the American male's tendency to leave women out of his real life—his business affairs. He tries to compensate by letting his wife and his daughters spend money indiscriminately, and his daughters thus develop the illusions that luxury is the proper expression of romance and that sentimental appeals are more effective than clear-sighted intelligence. With certain sophisticated variations this system also accounts for much of the confused thought of such figures as Nan St. George in *The Buccaneers* and even Lily Bart.

Insofar as "the custom of the country" creates in its products a simplification of moral issues, a sentimental disregard for the inflictions of experience, it has analogues in old New York, and both systems encourage that innocence against which Edith Wharton directs much of her moral indignation. In adapting to her own purposes the basic dichotomy of "the international novel"—American innocence set against European experience—she removes the subtle overtones of purity and guilt, focusing the contrast instead on simplistic evasion, and complex facing, of facts. So regarded, this dichotomy provides the essential base for her broad institutional contrasts of America and Europe, illustrated in stylized form by the juxtaposition of old New York and the Countess Olenska in *The Age of Innocence.* It is Ellen's very presence that gives meaning to the title, and her "experience" is constantly set against old New York's elevation of "factitious purity." Ellen's counterpart in this governing framework, May Welland, is presented in turn as "that terrifying product of the social system [Archer] belonged to and believed in, the young girl who knew nothing and expected everything" (p. 40). When such characters as May and Undine emerge primarily as "products," they tend to deflect our interests from personal to institutional matters, and what they do individually assumes the guise of social or class action.

Edith Wharton draws her secondary figures even more thoroughly as social types. As Lily Bart descends through the strata of New York society, for example, her progress is marked by association with such characters as the Dorsets, the Wellington Brys, the Ned Gormers, and Mrs. Norma Hatch, each of whom represents a class or a social development. Their behavior does not distinguish them personally; it categorizes them, just as the often comic details associated with them serve primarily to satirize a class. In analyzing such characters, Wharton is more interested in what they represent than in what they are.

Yet Wharton's focus on the social typicality of her characters produces many vivid secondary figures, the most interesting being Sillerton Jackson, Mrs. Manson Mingott, and Elmer Moffatt. On the one hand, the locating of representative qualities underscores the moral and sociological significance of the character and his manners, and on the other hand, in the context of the typical, small deviations can acutely mark the personal. Sillerton Jackson is Wharton's finest achievement at drawing an entirely representative character. He cannot be imagined apart from his society (he cannot even go to Newport!), and he strikes off old New York so perfectly that he can pass from *The Age of Innocence* to *New Year's Day* without losing his outline, his style, or his malicious power. His polish defines the tone of formal gatherings—the operas and dinners that are old New York's element as they are his own— just as his gossip reveals the underlying issues. As spokesman for New York's evaluations of persons, cuisine, manners and cigars, and as master of the art of innuendo, Jackson exercises great power, especially over Archer. But his power plays comically against his delicate measuring of personal comforts and his colorful idiom of judgment ("I didn't think the Mingotts would have tried it on"). The distinctive quality of Sillerton Jackson emerges, not in his deviation from "form," but in his relishing of it. His exquisite savoring of old New York's pleasures—famous Madeira and secret scandal—momentarily converts a stifling system into a mode of delight.

Mrs. Mingott, in contrast, distinguishes herself by a good many idiosyncrasies—living above Thirty-fourth Street in a house modeled on Parisian private hotels, playing the aged courtesan with younger men, embracing foreigners, and shocking New York by her "indecent propinquities" (her bedroom opens off her sitting room). But these minor audacities become idiosyncrasies only in the context of Mrs. Mingott's having remained within Fifth Avenue's major limits by her unsullied reputation for domestic fidelity and sexual propriety. Rather than be the foil of old New York, she represents one of its highest products, the eccentric who can play with convention while never threatening its framework. For all her sportiveness about Archer's attraction to Ellen, her eyes become "sharp as pen-knives" and her nails grasp his hand "like bird-claws" as she indirectly reminds Archer that he is erring from New York's code of domestic honor. The shrewdness that gave her power in her community is directed ultimately toward the preservation of that community.

But there is another side to Mrs. Mingott's eccentricity that affiliates her with an important group of Edith Wharton's secondary figures—a blunt, indecorous recognition of human nature. When Mrs. Welland objects "with the proper affectation of reluctance" to an early marriage for Archer and May, Mrs. Mingott's reply cuts through the pretense of polite manners: "Fiddlesticks!" In the novel of manners, with its dependence on polite evasion,

circumlocution, and tacit reference, there is an important role for
characters who speak the unspoken, and as their seemingly irrepressible honesty breaks through the conventional surface, such
characters show a peculiar vitality. Ordinarily their social positions
are less impregnable than Mrs. Mingott's, as in the case of the
socialite divorcée Carry Fisher, who not only tries to help Lily
Bart in her difficulties but often forces her to see them clearly.
And often they are frank interlopers, like Simon Rosedale and
Elmer Moffatt. As outsiders they see society without sentiment or
inherited attitudes, and although they miss a great deal, they
manage to articulate clearly certain issues that "gentlemen and
ladies" leave hazy.

Moffatt is the most energetic of these characters. Like most of
Wharton's secondary figures, he is primarily representative; from
his oppressive tangibility to his shrewd maneuvers, he embodies
the inevitable economic forces that destroy old New York and
make off with the outward manifestations of Old World culture.
But it is Moffatt's talk that vitalizes him and nearly offsets the
harsh judgment implied in his representative role. Unlike Undine
Spragg, who betrays her roots in Apex by unsuccessfully imitating
the speech of New Yorkers, Moffatt speaks the language of his
own past, and he blends this crude, forceful idiom with a blunt
appraisal of motive, as in replying to Undine's equivocations about
needing an annulment, "Then you think if you had the cash you
could fix it up all right with the Pope?" The language of polite
society may contain the resources for exacting and variable expression, as Wharton's own prose illustrates so well, but it is also
the medium of evasion and euphemism. Moffatt's robust vernacular
expresses an underlying honesty that survives even his transactions
in Wall Street. Indeed his swaggering defiance of the world and its
judgments is so distinctive, not only in *The Custom of the Country*
but in Wharton's whole range of fiction, that one wonders what
unacknowledged powers oversaw his conception.

Although Edith Wharton's three most interesting characters are
also "products" of social phenomena, they are substantial enough
to demand personal as well as sociological attention. Undine Spragg
stands out from all of Wharton's other protagonists by her boundless desire and self-assertion; she reveals the underside of Wharton's
characterization and tests the limits of her imagination. In Lily

Bart and Newland Archer, on the other hand, Wharton carries her investigation of manners to the back of the cave, showing how a social mask not only covers but recasts the buried self.

The Energy of Desire: Undine Spragg

Undine Spragg is the most perplexing of Edith Wharton's characters. She seems at once to provoke Wharton's laughter and to arouse her fear. Undine is obtuse, narrow, and egocentric; yet we see much of the story through her eyes. Why should a novelist concerned with the subtleties of perception and the complexities of behavior try to look at New York and France through such an unresponsive sensibility?

The problems Undine presents begin in her limitations. She has no soul, no inner life, no means of self-evaluation. The whole of reality for her is defined and sanctioned by the society page. She cannot recognize feelings in others that do not involve herself, and she cannot feel guilt over her own behavior. The only measure of her conduct, as she understands it, is whether she gets what she wants, and when others resist her she blames them, not herself. It is easy to judge such characteristics harshly because of the pain they produce in others, but Undine's childishness is in great part the result of her social typicality. She has been produced by "the custom of the country," spoiled since childhood, kept in ignorance of the relations between money and human activity, and overvalued in the eyes of others. It is hard to condemn Undine on moral grounds when so much of her behavior is dictated by her place in the sociological framework of the novel. She is caught between being an individual character, open to moral evaluation, and being the embodiment of a social phenomenon, demanding analysis more than personal judgment.

In Undine Wharton developed her most acute portrait of that strange being fabricated in the later nineteenth century—the American girl. Famed for her innocence, her extraordinary beauty and smart apparel, her personal freedom and rudeness with men, and her charming credulity, this object of wonder proliferated herself as myth over two continents while her real counterpart followed her on an aggressive campaign to acquire social position and personal effects. Through Undine Wharton shows that the rude, aggressive qualities are fostered by a social system that spoils young girls and deliberately creates the illusion that they deserve, and should be given, anything they desire. Undine's basic desires are so dependent on fluctuating popular tastes that she persists in credulity through a wide range of acquisitive experience—she simply wants amusement coexisting with respectability. Her innocence, then, is no basis for complacency in the American girl. Vain, blind to others' motives, and sexually impassive, she is exempt from what little she could recognize as temptation.

Undine's beauty causes another problem. She represents the physically idealized American girl, and men ranging from Elmer Moffatt to Raymond de Chelles respond so strongly to her beauty that we must believe in it. She lacks wit and intelligence, and her wealth is precarious; she depends for her success almost exclusively on her appearance. Yet Wharton will not allow us to accept Undine's beauty. In a world where the authorial norms require half-lights, shadings, and subtleties, Undine's element is the brightest glare of light, the waves of her hair are "glittering meshes," and when she wishes to be conspicuously attractive, she is "twitching," "fidgeting," and "restless." Wharton cannot describe Undine without revealing her own antipathy.

Despite her repugnant qualities and her limitations, however, Undine is a forceful and vivid character. What she lacks in self-awareness, sensibility, and intelligence, she more than compensates for by the abundance of one driving quality—desire. In fact, as regards Undine herself, *The Custom of the Country* is a narrative of desire. In each book of the novel, with the exception of the fourth, which deals exclusively with Ralph Marvell, Wharton constructs her narrative in the same basic pattern, a pattern determined by the nature and progress of desire. Undine begins with achievement. She has gotten what she wanted—life in a fashionable New York hotel, marriage to Ralph Marvell, freedom from him, marriage to Raymond de Chelles. But her triumph is coupled with disillusionment. Attaining her desires, she discovers, does not make her happy. In her West Side hotel she is ignored by fashionable New York; marriage to Ralph Marvell does not satisfy her longing to be in a conspicuous, brilliant society; rather than free her to marry Peter Van Degen, her divorce brings about social exclusion; and her marriage to Chelles seals her in a country estate when she wants most to be amused in Paris.

Released from its former object by such frustrations, her desire reasserts itself as a random, scattered, free-floating force. Undine enters a period of apprenticeship, during which she engages in the imitation of desire that I described in chapter 3. As she herself puts it, "I want what the others want," and in the ever-widening panorama of her social experience, she must repeatedly find out what the others do want and who the others are. *The Custom of the Country* has a more episodic structure than Wharton's other major novels, not because the narrative needs a panoramic scene for historical purposes, as in *The Valley of Decision*, but because in Wharton's analysis desire itself is episodic. Fulfillment is ironic in that it simply diverts Undine's desire into new channels, and exposure to more complicated experiences merely shows her how many more things there are to want. Given Undine's childish inability to pursue a distant object and her lack of ordered activities to fill in her time, she slips into utter aimlessness whenever she gets what she thought she wanted. The capricious movement of the narrative duplicates Undine's spurts of imitation as she tries to want and to do the "right thing." Should she get a Friday-night box at the opera, go for a ride in Central Park, see "the pictures" everyone is talking about, or buy a dinner dress? As long as Undine wants only things that, without too much effort, she can have, the narrative assumes the cyclic pattern that expresses Wharton's judgment and Undine's doom.

But Undine's bondage to a fixed pattern of desire does not preclude her from change, growth, or education. Her apprenticeship in desire coincides with a period of learning by imitation. Her sharp sense of surface detail and her outward adaptability give her a pure, hard power completely untroubled by comprehension. Thus her skill at imitating traditional speech and subdued manners initially deceives Ralph Marvell and conceals her utter blindness to his feelings and values. And he ought to know better, for his own theories about social change account for Undine precisely: the "invaders" acquire the speech of the "conquered race" without understanding its meanings. In fact, the English language dissolves into unintelligibility on Undine's tongue.

The limits on what she learns from imitation are more disturbingly reflected in what she learns from experience. If she cannot recognize an inner significance in manners, neither can she find a moral element in her own behavior. The problem goes beyond her stony indifference to the pain she inflicts on others. Undine is absolutely impervious to moral experience. Through all her frustrations she never learns what she ought to about her own course of life: that desire is self-generating, uncertain, and insatiable; that a life bent on the satisfaction of every desire turns through endless cycles of disillusioned success and aimless pursuit. Because she can neither curb her desires nor establish an order among them, she is the helpless prey of every new fashion and every social objective she encounters. Her life itself is wretched and she cannot tell why. What Undine does learn from defeat is more immediately practical. Especially after her major setback following her divorce from Ralph, she develops caution, prudence, and foresight. She learns to make plans, to dissimulate her intentions, and to exploit convention rather than be restrained by it. In short, although Undine learns nothing of value about desire itself, she becomes increasingly adept at fulfilling it.

In the last stages of her apprenticeship Undine's scattered wishes gradually consolidate themselves into a well-specified objective, and she escapes from aimlessness into a period of strategy. Her actions become coherent, and the narrative moves with the certainty of her intentions—to marry Ralph quickly, to divorce him and catch Peter Van Degen at the same time, to marry Chelles, or to exchange Saint Désert for Moffatt's millions. It is in this period that Undine is most unscrupulous, effective, and dangerous. She focuses all her arts and all that she has learned in her apprenticeship on her immediate purpose, but as she succeeds she enters a new cycle and must begin again.

These cycles of desire clarify and judge much of Undine's nature, and they reinforce the comic tone of the novel. From the detached vantage point implied by Wharton's satiric analysis, we watch Undine's antics with the assurance that she is finally bound in the narrow compass of her own nature. But Undine has energies not contained by the narrative comedy and not attributable to Wharton's mere disdain for the American girl and the Midwestern invaders. There is an edge of fear in her analysis; the caricature verges on nightmare. Although Undine is not Wharton's best character, she is certainly her most memorable, and Undine's curious power over the reader needs further explanation.

In characterizing Undine Spragg, Wharton took on a peculiar task that released creative energies not apparent elsewhere in her fiction. Not only did she objectify the social and personal qualities she most despised, but she imagined herself into them and thus had to call upon states of feeling that do not appear in her other novels. It is no accident that Undine is the only protagonist she projects with a genuine, almost boundless power of self-assertion. Given the deepest and most persistent values underlying Edith Wharton's fiction—continuity with the past, subordination of erratic impulses in a disciplined reverence for larger human achievement, the capacity to face experience honestly and to perceive the tangle of motives and restraints that make up the moral life—given these sources of worth in human existence, it is apparent that Undine Spragg is not only the inverse but the greatest threat to all that merits respect. She is virtually her creator's antiself. Blind to others' feelings and to moral experience, always preferring the new and the promiscuous to the old and the coherent, Undine emerges from Edith Wharton's imagination as the unbridled appetite in its purest form. She embodies everything that social institutions, at their most attractive, should check; and from any perspective but her own, and perhaps Moffatt's, the interest Undine arouses is as much in what can stop her as in what she can do.

Under the narrative of desire, then, lies a narrative of restraint, a testing of various social forms in their capacity to contain the individual appetite. Except in the face of the clearest sexual misbehavior—Undine's acceptance of a pearl necklace from Peter Van Degen while she is still Marvell's wife—her parents' Apex conventions never resist her; in fact, the Spraggs seem to regard their clearest duty as giving Undine what she wants. The manners of Washington Square depend so much on tacit assumption and evasion that they are little more effective than those of Apex. Ralph remains helpless before her because his social codes neither acknowledge such creatures as Undine nor offer principles and procedures to restrain them. Only in France does Undine find herself baffled and contained by a systematic force larger than herself. Not only does Raymond de Chelles have policy and obli-

gations to back up his will in resisting her, but his social codes
embody so much human experience that after he marries her he
can judge Undine for the child she is and treat her accordingly.

Coupled with her raw appetite, however, is an extraordinary
resilience in the face of defeat. This quality creates some moral
ambiguity in the narrative, especially in book 3. In the center of
this book, chapters 24 through 26, Undine's fortunes are at their
lowest point. She has divorced Ralph, and, as could be anticipated,
Van Degen has betrayed her. She has been snubbed in New York,
excluded from the circles she wants to enter in Europe, and left
with little money. Furthermore, there is something peculiarly
satisfying about the narrative at this point. Undine's fortunes and
social experiences coincide perfectly with our moral judgment.
As she slips from a circle of loose but respectable Americans to the
shady group surrounding the Baroness Adelschein, outward social
sanctions provide the exact measure of Undine's moral situation.
She is adequately judged. But this is only an outward and extreme
form of what occurs throughout the novel. As bad as Undine may
be, the reader is always consoled by a narrator whose judgment of
her is so clear, firm, and exacting that the reader need not be
troubled with further moral assessment. Wharton's very harshness
frees one to look at Undine without the distorting medium of
hatred.

It is with this liberation, augmented in book 3 by Undine's
outward punishment, that we witness her finest recovery. Frustrated and aimless, Undine is taken up by Raymond de Chelles's
frivolous cousin, the princess Estradina. She leads Undine on a
course of pleasure with the ultimate intention of steering her into
Chelles's arms as a lovely mistress to charm his bachelorhood.
Once Undine takes measure of the situation, she recoils with all
the indignation of "Apex puritanism." Her acute observations
during the period of failure, however, have taught her how to turn
the situation to her own advantage, and by allurement played
against resistance, she soon maneuvers Chelles into a proposal of
marriage. The sudden coldness of Lily Estradina and her associates
reveals their earlier intentions of turning a helpless American girl
to their own purposes. Insofar as this development contrasts
French and American manners, it makes Apex puritanism surprisingly attractive, and in recovering her powers of action after

a period of defeat, punishment, and exploitation, Undine almost becomes admirable.

What checks our admiration and effects the marriage is the intrusion of Elmer Moffatt with his plan to extort from Ralph and his family the money for Undine's annulment. Every time Undine reaches the critical moment in her strategy, Moffatt enters with the means by which her intentions can be realized; he exercises the ultimate force bringing about her transitions from one stage to the next. And these strong indications of his power are reinforced by Moffatt's more subtle effects on the quality of the narrative itself. Every time he appears, the meandering line of action suddenly becomes straight and coherent, at least for a time. If Undine is a free-floating threat to society, Moffatt provides the power and direction that make the threat effective. There have always been people with unchecked appetites; what makes Undine terrifying from the perspective of the entrenched classes is the set of powers dragged in the wake of her desires. Characteristically, Wharton amplifies individual problems by attaching them firmly to larger social changes, and once Moffatt's power backs Undine, the question shifts from how a social system can contain her impulses to how the system itself can survive her assault. In this sense Ralph Marvell serves primarily as an embodiment of the delicate adjustments that Undine destroys, a role that accounts both for his pathos and for his ineffectiveness as a character.

If there is any forward movement in the cyclical pattern of the novel, it is found in the increasing extent and complexity of Moffatt's actions in Undine's behalf. This movement reaches its appropriate culmination in their marriage. Beneath the snobbish and comic surface of *The Custom of the Country* Edith Wharton is projecting a vision of social cataclysm at the turn of the century— she sees uninformed, rapacious appetite converging with the titanic, amoral powers released in the most dizzying age of American capitalism. But Wharton's fascination with the forces that destroy what is most precious to her has here an ironic effect. Ordinarily this fascination leads her to represent social restraints with far more conviction than personal desires, but in *The Custom of the Country* it draws her attention to Undine and Moffatt themselves. Nothing Undine destroys is realized so compellingly as Undine herself; her frightening powers seem to involve more authorial fantasy than social prophecy. Undine has all the irrepressible energy of a bad dream, and Moffatt has all the power to make one's worst dreams come true.

A Dryad in the Drawing Room: Lily Bart

Lily Bart, too, emerges first as a social product; she represents the individual molded by the tastes and aspirations of a frivolous society, but given by her creator a sensibility too fine for its environment. She also typifies the girl with great beauty and the skill to enhance it but without money as a backing; she must maintain her social footing by personal arts alone. Lily's power as a character, however, derives from her inward resistance to her role and from Wharton's intense demands on her moral life. Lawrence Selden recognizes the first of these qualities at the out-set of the novel when he notes the "wild-wood grace" of Lily's outline, "as though she were a captured dryad subdued to the conventions of the drawing-room; and Selden reflected that it was the same streak of sylvan freedom in her nature that lent such savour to her artificiality" (p. 19). Lily's "savour" comes from a turbulent inner being that remains unsubdued by convention. If she wears her splendid social mask with less ease and more inward devastation than any of Edith Wharton's other characters, it is because in Lily Wharton projects psychic energies that are unmalleable to social forms.

Lily is the only major protagonist of whose physiological existence Wharton takes account. Ordinarily her fictions take place in a world of substantial objects and physically rarefied persons, and the sufferings of the characters are measured socially or inwardly. Lily can also suffer physically, and although the obvious examples of this at the end of the novel seem gratuitous, her physicality extends and complicates her inward nature. Her social dependency reaches into her sensory life. In order to exercise her discriminations and delicacies, she must be freed of physical needs in an atmosphere of elegance. Furthermore, Lily's social power depends finally on beauty and sexual allurement, and, as Wharton suggests by emphasizing Lily's age, these qualities are subject to decay. When Lily looks in a mirror, it is not, like Undine, to practice social gestures. Each of her anxieties leaves its trace on her appearance, and throughout the novel her plasticity and expressiveness harden into the lines of the outward mask she assumes at her most desperate moments. Her constant images of herself as a jewel are, in this context, deeply foreboding.

Her social mask is literal as well as figurative, and her outward appearance both reflects and intensifies her psychological experience. The latter, of course, is far more complicated; it is her psychological qualities that energize her. Years of social discipline, as Wharton frequently points out, cannot always master Lily's intuitive repugnances and passing impulses. Not only does her obscure inner self press Lily to indulge in "a natural thing," like visiting Selden's bachelor apartment; it forces her to recoil in disgust from the social artifice that could appease a dangerous witness, like Simon Rosedale. Yielding to either pressure, of course, is something Lily cannot afford, and the cost to her of each impulse measures the power of social sanctions and taboos. But if Lily's buried self threatens her social position and resists convention, her social experience itself distorts the impulses from beneath the surface. Early in the novel these impulses coincide roughly with the idealized version of Lily that Selden projects in describing the "republic of the spirit." The more Lily's social mask crystallizes under duress, however, the more her buried self becomes the agent of temptation. She finds herself chained to a terrifying second self which asks her to marry Simon Rosedale or to revenge herself on Bertha Dorset and which sends up "certain midnight images" that Lily must expunge from her consciousness. This transformation shows how ineluctably Lily's physical aging is attached to its psychological counterpart. The longer she maintains an artificial attitude, the more severe a strain she imposes on her inner nature. Each time she recovers her social poise by quelling her impulses, she reacts more quickly and with deeper disgust, and Wharton plots the stages of Lily's growing self-repugnance as precisely as she marks the steps of her social descent. Time means decay for Lily.

The conflict between society and self becomes in Lily's story a desperate battle between the public persona and the buried self, the one hardening in time and the other becoming more erratic and threatening. The wildness that savors Lily's artificiality is also,

then, the agent of resistance through which Wharton can show
what social convention does; but it is only part of what makes
Lily memorable as a character. If the struggle of two selves, recip-
rocally destroying each other, is a powerful spectacle, Wharton
intensifies and elevates Lily's situation by demanding that we
judge her conduct with the utmost moral seriousness. Although
Wharton acknowledges the devious psychological forces in Lily's
life, she does not abandon the moral analysis that psychological
narrative so often replaces. Lily's aging and decay appear not only
in lines on her face and in distortion of impulse, but more significantly in the deterioration of her moral fiber. Each new compromise
between impulse and convention weakens her ability to withstand
temptation, and each new image or idea that she learns under
pressure to live with marks a moral decline.

Nowhere does Edith Wharton reveal her admiration of Balzac
more clearly than in her characterization of Lily Bart. She demands
moral integrity in precisely those social circumstances where one
is least likely to find it. Like Balzac, she gives moral weight to her
heroine by analyzing her under extraordinary pressures—financial
need, vanity, ambition, impulse, social expectation—and she illuminates each stage of moral compromise. Again like Balzac, she
maximizes Lily's temptations by placing them at the moments
when her needs are greatest and her inward resistance most
weakened. In these moments of stress Wharton never lets us forget
the moral issues. She sees them more clearly and more consistently
than her heroine, Lily's thinking often being blurred by her small
benevolences, her restored vanity, a new income, or a change of
scene. And Wharton analyzes the issues in a language more abstract,
firm, and penetrating than could reflect Lily's own understanding.
But she holds Lily accountable for her conduct by precisely defining her character in a moral context: "In her inmost heart Lily
knew it was not by appealing to the fraternal instinct that she was
likely to move Gus Trenor; but this way of explaining the situation
helped to drape its crudity, and she was always scrupulous about
keeping up appearances to herself. Her personal fastidiousness had
a moral equivalent, and when she made a tour of inspection in her
own mind there were certain closed doors she did not open"
(p. 131). And when Lily herself is forced by outward failure to
examine her situation, she not only recognizes its probable conse-

quences but acknowledges her own moral complicity in producing it. Thus, while Wharton's analysis lends moral significance to the manners of a trivial society, Lily's own contemplation of her actions defines her as a serious moral agent. The following passage, dealing with Lily's disastrous Mediterranean cruise, illustrates how author and heroine reinforce each other in giving moral weight to the story:

For though she knew she had been ruthlessly sacrificed to Bertha Dorset's determination to win back her husband, and though her own relation to Dorset had been that of the merest good-fellowship, yet she had been perfectly aware from the outset that her part in the affair was, as Carry Fisher brutally put it, to distract Dorset's attention from his wife. That was what she was "there for": it was the price she had chosen to pay for three months of luxury and freedom from care. Her habit of resolutely facing the facts, in her rare moments of introspection, did not now allow her to put any false gloss on the situation. She had suffered for the very faithfulness with which she had carried out her part of the tacit compact, but the part was not a handsome one at best, and she saw it now in all the ugliness of failure. [pp. 365-66]

This passage, however, culminates one line of development in the novel, just as the public crisis motivating these reflections terminates Lily's social power. Lily has been acting with deliberate choice or with hazy motives that she soon sees clearly, and she knows that she is responsible for what she has done, despite the pressures on her. Furthermore, Wharton's rhetorical strategies accentuate Lily's own part in her actions. From the opening pages of the novel we are encouraged, through Lawrence Selden's point of view, to use the "argument from design" in interpreting Lily's conduct. To him each of her acts seems purposeful: she deals with people on the basis of "far-reaching intentions," and even in unforeseen circumstances she improvises skillfully, making full use of the material at hand. The narrative in book 1 supports his analysis. In the first eight chapters we see Lily in four major personal encounters—with Selden, Percy Gryce, Gus Trenor, and Simon Rosedale. The common element of these episodes is that they illustrate Lily's skillful tactics directed at a specific purpose. It is true that each of these encounters marks a moral step downward, that in each case Lily's control becomes more desperately a means of extrication from difficulties she has created in earlier encounters, but this is simply to say that we are witnessing serious moral action by an agent not only deliberate but clever. She makes choices and defines herself further by each one, and she discovers parts of her finer nature each time she shrinks from baseness or faces inwardly what she has done.

After Bertha dismisses Lily from the yacht, however, the narrative changes fundamentally. Again Selden's meditations signal the kind of interest we bring to the narrative. At the outset of book 2 he compares the social scene on the Riviera to a stage set for the closing tableau of a drama with the performance intensified by "the hovering threat of the curtain." Instead of scrutinizing what Lily does, trying to discern the thread of intention, we are now simply to watch what happens, that is, what happens *to* Lily before the final curtain. And the series of major episodes that open this book form a tight sequence illustrating Lily's loss of refuge and protection. The spectacle differs markedly from that in book 1: Lily no longer demonstrates her social arts by manipulating other people; the best she can do is to preserve appearances. If this change in Lily, from action to sufferance and reaction, were to measure the effects of her former compromises, the story would maintain its moral firmness; but Bertha's antagonism, which triggers Lily's other setbacks, bears little relationship to what Lily herself has done. Lily changes, in other words, from a complex individual, making choices and facing their consequences, into an agent of the plot, a figure doomed and pursued by the implacable furies. As she slips from the Brys to the Gormers to Mrs. Norma Hatch to the milliner's shop, Lily loses more and more of her original outline, succumbing less to the pressures of her environment than to Wharton's relentless conception of what happens to a fine character in a crass society. It is disturbing to see Lily destroyed, but it is far more disturbing to see Wharton change Lily's qualities and make her destruction so largely arbitrary; it defeats the expectations created by book 1.

Lily does manage to preserve two of her major qualities, an aversion to dinginess and just enough moral integrity not to use the blackmail letters. But in book 2 the aversion to dinginess becomes a stock response, and the moral integrity stiffens into a hard and fixed imperative, no longer subject to the subtle flexibility and variety of application it had when Lily was simultaneously growing and decaying with her actions. The crystallization of these qualities shows how the vivid and substantial Lily Bart of book 1 is dying long before her literal death. In fact, what Wharton implies is that outside the society that produced her, Lily necessarily ceases to exist; she has no core of self that can establish new relations with a larger world:

> She had learned by experience that she had neither the aptitude nor the moral constancy to remake her life on new lines; to become a worker among workers, and let the world of luxury and pleasure sweep by her unregarded. She could not hold herself much to blame for this ineffectiveness, and she was perhaps less to blame than she believed. Inherited tendencies had combined with early training to make her the highly specialized product she was: an organism as helpless out of its narrow range as the sea-anemone torn from the rock. She had been fashioned to adorn and delight; to what other end does nature round the rose-leaf and paint the humming-bird's breast? [pp. 486-87]

In this passage Wharton shows what has happened to Lily in the course of the narrative: the individual, morally responsible character has been sacrificed to her creator's concern with social determinism. Such a discussion explicitly deflects the moral evaluation that Wharton's earlier analyses had encouraged. She finds herself caught between developing a character and portraying the society that shapes the character, and she habitually chooses the latter.

In this regard her comments on how she conceived *The House of Mirth* are illuminating:

> The problem was how to extract from such a subject [fashionable New York] the typical human significance which is the story-teller's reason for telling one story rather than another. In what aspect could a society of irresponsible pleasure-seekers be said to have, on the "old woe of the world", any deeper bearing than the people composing such a society could guess? The answer was that a frivolous society can acquire dramatic significance only through what its frivolity destroys. Its tragic implication lies in its power of debasing people and ideals. The answer, in short, was my heroine, Lily Bart.[2]

Lily, in other words, is simply the means by which Wharton can give significance to her social portrait, a character created for the needs of a particular kind of story. Once she leaves the social milieu that is Wharton's real subject, her only remaining function

---

[2] *A Backward Glance*, p. 207.

is to be destroyed. And here again we come upon the essential difference between the kinds of fiction written by Edith Wharton and Henry James. In his preface to *The Portrait of a Lady*, he, too, discusses the problem of subject:

By what process of logical accretion was this slight "personality," the mere slim shade of an intelligent but presumptuous girl, to find itself endowed with the high attributes of a Subject?—and indeed by what thinness, at the best, would such a subject not be vitiated? Millions of presumptuous girls, intelligent or not intelligent, daily affront their destiny, and what is it open to their destiny to *be*, at the most, that we should make an ado about it? . . . Therefore, consciously, that was what one was in for—for positively organising an ado about Isabel Archer.[3]

His subject is not only Isabel's destiny but Isabel herself, and he likes his heroine too much to sacrifice any interest she might possess to his delineation of her surroundings. Wharton, on the other hand, likes Lily Bart too much to believe that she can endure, much less succeed, in the world as given. That the spectacle of Lily's destruction haunts one's memory is primarily due to Wharton's earlier seriousness about her as a psychologically and morally substantial being. There is something repugnant about comparing Lily Bart to a sea anemone.

Prisoner of a Hackneyed Vacabulary
Newland Archer

Edith Wharton does not sacrifice her finest character, Newland Archer, to the social portrait, for the two are inseparable; when he is most individual, he displays the most extensive and complex ties to his community. In characterizing Archer, Wharton achieved the purest and most distinctive expression of her narrative art. Nowhere else does she probe so subtly and thoroughly the central subject of her fiction—the correspondence of outward convention and inward experience. The assumptions governing her characterization of Archer differ markedly from those behind Lily Bart. For Lily the impulsive life stands out sharply against social discipline, and the latter involves self-conscious control. These

[3]*Portrait*, I, xii-xiii.

well-defined forces struggle dramatically throughout her story.
Archer's story is far subtler, less striking to the imagination. In it
Wharton develops a different notion of social discipline, more
peculiarly her own and ultimately more disconcerting. No longer
an acquired art deliberately exercised, it now appears as the
acquired *nature* of the social being. Instead of checking the inward
self at critical moments and distorting impulse by resistance, social
convention pervades the mind constantly, shaping its activities and
governing the very experience of an impulse. Archer cannot define,
as clearly as Lily can, either his own desires or the discipline that
checks them; he goes through more confusion than conflict.

The issue of Archer's development, then, is how many of his
concealed impulses and habitudes he can bring into consciousness
without losing his coherence. Insofar as he does grow, it is by the
enrichment of his inner life, but the process is difficult, and the
barriers to self-knowledge reveal the psychological effects of manners. On the one hand, Archer's sense of identity depends so much
on the habits and assumptions of old New York that new attitudes
threaten his stability. On the other hand, his impulsive life has been
so concealed and stereotyped by a conventional vocabulary that
he can scarcely know, much less trust, what he feels. When Ellen
Olenska simultaneously releases in him a new awareness of his conventions as merely conventions and a new appreciation of internal
possibilities, Archer's old personality breaks up. As he looks
outward to other social arrangements and inward to a fuller realization of himself, both his social and his psychological identities
begin to drift. Although the two sides of his growth are subtly
related to each other, each is so demanding and difficult in the
social context that Archer can deal consciously with only one kind
of experience at a time. While he attends to his gradual detachment
from his society, he remains unconscious of his growing attraction
to Ellen; and when he concentrates on his feelings about her, he
loses sight of the activities and the significance of his public world.
Only in the concluding chapter can Archer assimilate both kinds
of experience, recognize their interdependence, and thus reintegrate
himself.

The structure of the novel reflects the segmentation of Archer's
growth. In book 1 he is explicitly engaged in examining his settled
convictions, and his impulsive life develops unregarded. In book 2

he has recognized his inner needs, but in focusing on them he forgets about their relationship to his social habits. Yet both kinds of experience develop simultaneously, and thus Archer's psychological progress appears in two forms of indirection. Concerning the subject of his conscious interest—his social identity in book 1 and his inward possibilities in book 2—his development is reflected in his ways of thinking: his handling of his settled convictions or his projecting of new relations with Ellen Olenska. His unconscious development appears at a further remove; it governs the images he projects and the hiatuses and irrational moves in his conscious thought. More importantly, it confuses and warps the conscious development itself, demonstrating the interdependence of his social and his psychological identities. Thus his illicit attraction to Ellen in book 1 interferes with his thoughts about New York, and his social conventions, disregarded in book 2, threaten to debase his feelings about Ellen. Archer's psychic state, then, is projected in his images of himself and others, and since the novel centers on his consciousness, the shifting qualities attributed to Ellen and May actually serve to characterize Archer himself. It is tempting to regard Ellen as the projection of his inner possibilities and May as the agent of the outward conventions he is examining. His choice of one or the other woman would then represent his acknowledgment of one area of experience as finally more significant. But this temptation to simplify and schematize is precisely Archer's problem.

To confront directly the issues of Archer's development, one must begin with the question, What *is* each of these women to Archer, and what *can* she be? As a foreigner Ellen represents two quite distinct worlds for Archer—a world of social arrangements that encourage free movement through all areas of experience and a world of moral complications beyond the safe limits of old New York. Her experience both attracts Archer's envy and arouses his indignation. May represents the counterpart of each world—a social world of arbitrary restrictions and a moral world of "peace, stability, comradeship, and the steadying sense of an unescapable duty." The schematization of the two women is thus doubled by a split in Archer's conception of each one. The conventional sources and the psychological effects of this splitting are more extensively developed through the image of the Countess Olenska, for Archer devotes more of his conscious and unconscious energies to her. I will return, however, to the cost of his disregard for May.

Although Ellen initiates both Archer's social and psychological growth, he can cope with only one at a time, and thus he projects alternate images: one of Ellen as socially familiar with artists and writers, the other of the "disgraced" Countess who has suffered unimaginable cruelties and who has probably compromised herself to escape them. The version of her that he accepts at a given moment corresponds to the nature of his affiliation with her—if she is the disgraced Countess, he is her rescuer or, unconsciously, her would-be seducer; if she is the habituée of European salons, he is the novitiate in a wider social world. Ellen's sexual and cultural richness are, of course, counterparts of each other, and to see her humanly Archer would have to accept both images simultaneously and adjust them to each other. But everything in his acquired nature works against such a harmonious and complete view.

In the first place the shock of her attitudes about New York fills the foreground of Archer's consciousness with uncertainties about his basic principles. His ensuing confusion is apparent when the Mingott clan names him "legal adviser" to discourage Ellen from divorce. Here the narrative illustrates Wharton's methods of handling the barriers to Archer's conscious thought. True to his background, he does not want to see the details and innuendoes of the legal documents, and once he does, he takes the standard view that the divorce would create "unpleasant" publicity. Then, in conference with his legal superior, he rebels against the narrowness of his conventions. It is not sympathy with her case but dissatisfaction with his own assumptions that leads Archer to attempt giving Ellen an impartial hearing. But when she can give no satisfactory reason for wishing a divorce, Archer falls back into New York's suspicions about her attachment to Count Olenski's secretary. These suspicions are abetted by impulsive pressures of which Archer is unaware. His sense of triumph when Ellen dismisses Beaufort to talk with him alone shows him to be jealous of her private life, just as his thoughts about her fur-collared gown and her bare arms reveal his sexual excitement. Thus when she remains silent at his implications about the secretary, he not only believes them but feels personally thwarted. He argues the New

York case in all its platitudes, then, not because he believes in it, but because it allows him to conceal and circumvent his unacceptable feelings. Such sequences of reactions, tangled motives, and evasions characterize the conventional impediments to Archer's thinking and show how disregarded impulses help shape his deliberation.

In the second place his manners block him from an integrated view of Ellen and of himself by concealing and codifying his impulses. Yet Wharton manages to trace the development of these impulses behind Archer's back, and in doing so she probes most deeply the effects of convention on the soul. Her first method is to arrange significantly the dark intervals in Archer's conscious thought. The drama of the opening scene, for example, occurs primarily in the erratic movement of Archer's mind. As he watches Mme. Nilsson on stage and May in the Mingott box, he anticipates his manly privilege of initiating his betrothed. But the thought of her "abysmal purity" leads him to wish that she should at once retain the strength of purity and become worldly wise, that she should be a "miracle of fire and ice." He cannot get beyond this contradiction, for he recognizes that everyone in the club box shares his ideal, and he turns his attention to "masculine New York," first recognizing its uniformity, then feeling his own intellectual superiority, and finally acknowledging his acquiescence on all moral issues. Curiously, he elaborates on this last idea, feeling that on moral questions it would be "troublesome—and also rather bad form—to strike out for himself." In the hiatuses of this sequence, it is apparent that Archer actually is striking out for himself, tentatively and unconsciously. He is chafing at the restraints of his own conventionality, and when he diverts his thoughts from the contradiction of fire and ice, his hidden impulses cluster about the unexplained element—the source of "fire" in May's potential nature. And precisely when his inward emphasis on club-box morality checks his errant impulses, the whole interior drama moves out into public view, as the outward projection of "fire"—Ellen Olenska—joins the outward projection of "ice" in the Mingott box. No wonder Archer is thrown into "a strange state of embarrassment" by this episode; it is too close to home.

Wharton's major way of projecting Archer's unacknowledged impulses is through the very images he confronts. Throughout book 1 she employs the symbolic dichotomies of nineteenth-century romance—brunette and blonde heroines, fire and ice, vibrant roses and pale lilies, painful flushes and crystalline clarity—which were themselves conventions for suggesting the kind of impulsive conflict that Archer is experiencing. They have a more complicated appropriateness to Archer in book 1, for New York's conventions are not the only ones that have shaped his inner life. He has seen enough plays and read enough poetry and fiction to have literary sanctions for feelings not cultivated in New York. But these feelings are themselves warped by his social habits, for New York makes such a cleavage between literature and life that it seems impossible to experience for oneself the feelings one reads about. As May so aptly puts it, "We can't behave like people in novels, though, can we?" This is not to deny the existence of certain feelings, merely their legitimacy. Although Archer knows the sequences of action and passion in many literary works, he cannot accept this knowledge as pertinent to his own experience. He does not know how much he knows, and by denying his knowledge of "unusual situations," he allows the feelings and suspicions modeled on illicit stories to rampage through his mind without acknowledgment, much less control. His already fragmented image of Ellen, then, is overlaid with miscellaneous associations from his reading, as when Rossetti's *The House of Life* affirms his most ineffable feelings about her and provides the phrase that consecrates all he has missed—"the flower of life."

But Archer's major unconscious literary model projects onto Ellen an image that severely threatens their relationship. It begins with his decision to "champion" and then to "rescue" Ellen when rumor indicates that she may damage May's reputation. To rescue her presupposes a threat, and once she has the social blessing of old New York, the threat can no longer be seen in the disapprobation of the club box. Through the influence of social innuendo and his own reading, Archer postulates a sexual threat, and Ellen becomes the stock figure of Gothic fantasy—the pursued maiden. Again New York's accepted judgments suggest to Archer who the dark pursuer may be—Julius Beaufort. Throughout book 1 he appears with Ellen whenever Archer himself is approaching her with unconscious sexual impulses. Beaufort's role is clearest at Skuytercliff, where Archer follows Ellen after she "runs away"

from New York to feel "safe." When Archer chases her down on
the snow-covered landscape, he appears himself as the pursuer, but
he persists in projecting his desires onto other figures, such as a
"dark menace from abroad." Inside the Patroon's house he asks
her who she is running from, while his own heart beats insubordi-
nately.

> For a long moment she was silent; and in that moment Archer imagined her,
> almost heard her, stealing up behind him to throw her light arms about his
> neck. While he waited, soul and body throbbing with the miracle to come,
> his eyes mechanically received the image of a heavily-coated man with his
> fur collar turned up who was advancing along the path to the house. The man
> was Julius Beaufort. [pp. 133-34]

The "image" here seems to arise directly from the movement of
Archer's fantasies; Beaufort virtually projects Archer's shadow self.
But because Beaufort himself is well known in New York, Archer's
disgust at his appearance allows him again to evade his own feelings.
As long as Ellen appears to him as the pursued maiden, his own
feelings for her can themselves only be of a forbidden sort.

Thus through most of book 1 the course of Archer's fantasy life
is hidden from his view, and the conventions of his society and of
his reading govern his unconscious ties to Ellen. After May intuits
that Archer may love someone else, and after Archer himself
declares his love to Ellen, he begins to unearth his impulsive life.
Once he acknowledges that he has a relationship with Ellen, he can
begin to concentrate on what that relationship is to be. This is the
subject of his conscious thought in most of book 2. But again his
social habits impair his development, no longer by concealing his
desires but by tempting him to place himself and Ellen in familiar
categories. Their relationship undergoes two basic changes in
quality during book 2. The first occurs when they meet in Boston.
Outside the world in which "sophisticated witnesses" would make
Archer play a role and see his meeting as a failure in "any current
valuation," he can forget the conventional footing of relationships
and regard himself and Ellen as human beings. And Ellen here
makes their relationship so natural and honest that they can accept
and balance both their own feelings and their obligations to others.

But this balance is tense, and the strong sexual attraction that
invigorates it can be sublimated only when Archer rises above the
suspicions and habits of his class. When they resume their relations

in New York, Archer succumbs to the residual feelings associated with Ellen as pursued maiden, and he articulates these feelings in the only vocabulary available, that of old New York's game of masculine sexuality. Although this game is disgustingly familiar to him, so familiar that he knows it will debase and finally destroy their relationship, it seems to provide the only pattern within which he can acknowledge his feelings, and he presses Ellen toward a conventional liaison. It could be argued, then, that May's intervention saves, rather than destroys, their special bond.

While Archer's relationship to Ellen occupies the foreground of his conscious life, May and New York seem to him distant, frozen, and unreal. The very subjects that had excluded Ellen and his inward life in book 1 are themselves submerged in book 2 by his obsession with his newly discovered feelings. He assumes that because he found the surface of his life monotonous, it will never change. But it does change. As his desires and associations move unseen in the background of book 1, so May and her allied social forces act in the background in book 2, pressuring Ellen to stay away from New York and finally compelling her return to Europe. From the moment May intuits his uncertainties about another woman, it is apparent that Archer has underestimated her, that he has accepted the convention of feminine innocence too simply. Thus, whereas the three chapters culminating the main narrative seem to Archer to trace the moves in a "deadly serious game" between Ellen and himself, a game in which he holds the "trump card" of leaving May irrevocably, the effective action in these chapters involves May's triumph in ejecting Ellen.

Archer's blindness to May's skillful activity has, however, more serious consequences to him. Her skill is part of her complexity, her human reality, and throughout their married life Archer never recognizes who she is. If the schematization of Ellen and May retards his acceptance of Ellen in her full reality, it destroys his capacity to understand May. Long after Wharton has discarded the conventional devices of the romance in characterizing Ellen, she indicates that Archer continues to associate May with the icy purity of Diana. May holds her conventional shape in Archer's mind from the opening scene of "a young girl in white with eyes ecstatically fixed on the stage-lovers" to the closing phrase of the main narrative, "her blue eyes wet with victory." For a mind

formed by New York's manners and by conventional reading, it
may be difficult to discern reality through the screen of the exotic,
but it is virtually impossible to pierce the mask of what is most
familiar.

The lapse of twenty-six years before the concluding chapter, an
interval in which old New York and its manners have outwardly
disappeared, provides a shift of perspective that is crucial in evalu-
ating Archer's story. Ironically, he learns of May's inner complexity
through the submergence of the very habits that made his story
significant. Long after May herself is dead, Archer's son, unre-
strained by his parents' delicacies, casually tells him about May's
last words. And once Archer knows that she was fully aware of his
sacrifice, he knows something else his son cannot discern—that she
interpreted his fidelity through a code that made it important.
To Dallas, of course, Archer's renunciation was simply "a pathetic
instance of vain frustration." On the one hand, then, Wharton
accentuates the subtlety of Archer's story by refracting it in the
mind of one for whom it seems an old-fashioned vagary. On the
other hand, Archer's long effort to reintegrate himself, to come to
terms with both his inner needs and his outward sanctions, has
culminated in a period when the very vocabulary of those sanctions
has been superseded. Whatever meaning he can find in his past
must exist only in his mind. Yet the changes in New York itself
give Archer a field of meditation on which he can demonstrate
the serene and flexible inner vision that has emerged through his
outward renunciation. As he balances the dignity, restraint, and
coherence of the old order against the spontaneity, openness, and
confidence of the new, as he does this with compassion but
without bitterness, he vindicates his nearly disastrous relationship
with Ellen Olenska. For at her best she was the agent simultaneously of the wider life that Archer craved and of the honest
confrontation with reality that he did not know he needed.

It seems appropriate that Wharton's finest character and her
fullest examination of the inner life should both emerge from the
novel in which she creates the most well-defined social order. Both
the structure of Archer's inner world and the emergence of his
identity depend on the sanctions and manners of old New York.
Whatever significance he and the reader can find in his relinquish-
ment appears first in the special context of old New York's values—

scrupulousness about behavior, delicacy in conversation and therefore in perception, and an awesome sense of obligation. But if these values dignify Archer's story, the manners that preserve and transmit them have made Archer himself pitiable. The confusion, blindness, and irrelevant temptation through which he painfully makes his way do not characterize personal weaknesses so much as predispositions shaped by outward manners. What is most disturbing about the phenomenon of Newland Archer, however, is the broader conception of human existence underlying his story. If the individual is as inwardly determined by local manners as Newland Archer, it matters little whether he comes from old New York or from Apex City; he is going to miss "the flower of life." Furthermore, we cannot dismiss Wharton's determinism as an easy formula or a quirk of temperament; she shows far too much intelligence, moral subtlety, and precise observation for us to evade her implications. And finally, the determinism is not so overt as to make Archer morally negligible; it exists rather as a cluster of inward tendencies in an agent otherwise both sensitive and morally intelligent. It is difficult to fault either the understanding or the moral seriousness informing Wharton's portrait of Newland Archer, and yet to accept what she says makes one feel somehow smaller.

Society and the Empty Core

Two tendencies, then, predominate in Wharton's characterization. She develops the inner life primarily through the quality and changes of a character's perceptions, usually testing these on questions of social behavior. Outwardly she draws her characters as products of social class or social change. Both methods deflect our attention from the characters themselves to what they think about or represent—social phenomena. In Wharton's fiction we are confronted on the one hand with precisely observed manners and the assumptions underlying them; on the other, with acute reflections, analyses, and generalizations. The detail and the concept may often stand in clear relationship to each other, but between them one misses fundamental aspects of character. Wharton's central figures, with the notable exception of Undine, suffer from a defect of will, and all of them have ineffective imaginations. Vague and insubstantial, their aspirations neither move the reader nor excite their own wills to action. Wharton's sympathetic characters find themselves trapped not only by sentiment but by an absence of force in pursuing their ideals and interests.

Furthermore, Wharton's characters are diminished by her inability to project their emotional lives with conviction. She seems to have a stoic distrust of passion itself, finding nobility only in its ravages, and she often caricatures emotion as the source and evidence of self-deception. When she engages her men and women in romantic scenes, she reverts to the easiest of emotional counters—throbs, electrical flashes, changes of color, warm currents. Except for those feelings associated with loss or defeat, which are extraordinarily moving in her fiction, she conveys emotion in spongy, inconsequential language.

By making her minor characters primarily embodiments of social types and by failing to develop a variety of personal relationships, Wharton reduces the complex connections among human beings to a confrontation between the protagonist and the fragments of his society. For such novelists as Balzac and Jane Austen, society emerges as the clustering of several individually realized beings, related to each other in a variety of ways: in Austen's novels society is simply the sum of the actual and potential relationships entered into by individuals. For Wharton the notion of society comes first; we feel the power of old New York before we accept the individual force of Sillerton Jackson. Although the complexity of an individual's ties with society itself has rarely seen more acute fictional examination, Wharton stylizes and reduces that other kind of complexity which arises from the interlocking personal ties among several individuals. And since each well-developed relationship to one other character brings out new aspects of the identity and quality of the protagonist, Wharton's deflection of personal to social ties amounts to a diminishing of the individual substance and variety her protagonists can have.

If the minor characters embody parts of society, the major characters reflect on, and raise questions about, social problems. The issues and narrative procedures that vitalize Undine, Lily, and Archer as individuals invariably turn on the relationship between outward manners and the individual. That is, even when Wharton succeeds in drawing a substantial character, the very qualities informing that individuality raise questions ultimately of a social nature, and her best characters seem designed to dramatize such problems rather than to live their own lives. Her interest in perception abets this tendency by turning details of behavior and scene into aspects of characterization. She follows her own precept in *The Writing of Fiction* that the impression of outward circumstances should constitute an event in the protagonist's soul. Most of her central characters tend to become centers of perception and observation; and since she sees no clear bounds on the individual personality but instead an imperceptible flowing into adjacent persons and things, the more her characters see, the more they dissolve into what they see. The final effect of Wharton's characterization is to emphasize two things: the substance of social behavior and the mind working with it. And the impressiveness of that mind characterizes not her fictional people but Edith Wharton herself.

Chapter V

Analytic Style
The Filtering of Judgment

IN CONFRONTING THE problems discussed in the preceding chapters, one makes the loose but convenient assumption that a novelist's words on the page serve as a transparency through which one observes actions, societies, manners, or living persons. But the words also stand between us and the fictional world. They establish the categories within which the actions appear to us, and their arrangement in sentences orders the immediate movement of our thoughts and feelings. An author's phrasing is his most intimate way of creating the sort of reader his fiction needs. Occasionally novelists manipulate or experiment with their language to such an extent as to make the medium perceptible, and when narrative language becomes interesting in itself, the novelist is obviously and deliberately asking his reader to explore the relation of language to experience. But more often style in prose fiction seems subservient to story, character, and theme; and its effects, not being sharply marked, easily go unnoticed. This is especially true for Edith Wharton, who had, as she puts it, "a reverence for the English language as spoken according to the best usage." Her lucid and flexible narrative language illustrates her respect for the capacities of traditional English prose. She tries to make words on the page function as neither more nor less than a medium of rational communication.

This tells little, however, about the immediate effects of Wharton's style. To recognize these, we must look further into the distinction between language as a transparency and language as an opaque and definitive medium. This distinction arises in the act of perception.[1] In a welter of sense impressions we perceive objects,

---

[1] In formulating the theoretical base of my analysis, I have been guided in part by Richard M. Ohmann's discussions of prose style. See especially "Prolegomena to the Analysis of Prose Style," in *Style in Prose Fiction,* English Institute Essays, 1958, ed. H. C. Martin (New York, 1959); and *Shaw: The Style and the Man* (Middletown, Conn., 1962).

actions, and meaningful clusters in part because we impose certain forms on our experience. Language provides some of the most important of these forms. We perceive different things, for example, if every tree has its own name than we do if we impose the word *tree* on several distinct clusters of sensation. Our diction represents our ways of categorizing experience. Our syntax, in turn, discloses the kinds of relationships and activities we characteristically recognize; it shows how we order our experience. Through the causal or concessive aspects of syntax, we discover or posit more refined relationships than we do with the connective *and*. An author's syntactic habits, then, tell us how he sees. These habits also condition the reader's perception, encouraging him first to accept and later to seek out the kinds of connections the author makes. Language is transparent in referring outward to the world we perceive, to a fact or cluster of facts that could, theoretically, be verified. It is opaque in determining the way in which we grasp those facts. The reordering of parts within a sentence need not alter the external circumstances to which the sentence refers, but it changes the succession of expectancies through which we apprehend those circumstances. The transparency of language expresses our sense that the author could have said what he said in slightly different ways; the opacity arises from the fact that he chose *this* way.

Let me illustrate the distinction with a sentence from *The House of Mirth:* "An impulse of curiosity made him turn out of his direct line to the door, and stroll past her." Here is another sentence specifying the same circumstances: "He turned out of his direct line to the door and strolled past her, impelled by curiosity." Insofar as language is a transparency, these two sentences say the same thing, and my substitute tells us very nearly as much as the original about Selden and his action. But not quite. Wharton's choice makes an abstraction into the active agent and places Selden's direct action on a plane of discrimination, governed by a preceding moral phrase. Her Selden is slightly less responsible than mine, and his activity is more subject to refined contemplation than to simple observation. These attendant meanings make up the effects of style, and they gather great force in a narrative when the stylistic choices creating them are recurrent enough, as in the present example, to constitute a basic trait of the narrative language.

   The following discussion is an attempt to describe these covert
meanings in Edith Wharton's prose, to elucidate the preconcep-
tions, attitudes, and expectations she forces us to entertain by her
diction, phrasing, and sentence structure. Some of the distinctive
stylistic qualities I describe are general enough to pertain to the
prose throughout her canon, but her style changes in important
ways, and to make these changes intelligible in the three major
novels, I have had to exclude much of the complicating evidence
offered by her other novels. Developmentally, for example, *The
Glimpses of the Moon* bears surprisingly little stylistic resemblance
to *The Age of Innocence*, even though it was written at very nearly
the same time in her career, and a generalization encompassing
both books would simply be too broad to be helpful. The justification for my procedure is that it distinguishes the stylistic
peculiarities of her three most important books, *The House of
Mirth, The Custom of the Country,* and *The Age of Innocence*.
I do not discuss the weaknesses of her writing in such novels as
The Glimpses of the Moon and *The Gods Arrive* for a similar
reason—I am trying not to assess her style aesthetically but to
account for the stylistic implications of her prose at its most
powerful.

Diction and Categorizing

The peculiarities of Wharton's diction are most striking in her early
prose. The following passage from *The House of Mirth*, describing
Lily's analysis of the Trenor circle when Selden has opened a new
perspective for her, illustrates the problems raised by the categories
of Wharton's language:

Lily smiled at her classification of her friends. How different they had seemed
to her a few hours ago! Then they had symbolized what she was gaining, now
they stood for what she was giving up. That very afternoon they had seemed
full of brilliant qualities; now she saw that they were merely dull in a loud
way. Under the glitter of their opportunities she saw the poverty of their
achievement. It was not that she wanted them to be more disinterested; but
she would have liked them to be more picturesque. And she had a shamed
recollection of the way in which, a few hours since, she had felt the centri-
petal force of their standards. [p. 88]

The phrasing here is balanced almost to the point of sounding stilted. In successive sentences Wharton probes the distinction between the promise and the actuality of Lily's society, each sentence offering another aspect of the contrast. Moving from Lily's own relation to her circle, the passage ascends to a highly generalized judgment of the society itself. The emphatic balancing draws attention to the gulf between the Trenor circle's activities and the desires of Lily's finer self.

But there is another gulf in this passage. If Lily makes spiritual and aesthetic demands on a frivolous society, Wharton makes moral ones. The vocabulary resounds with moral judgment—"giving up," "opportunities," "achievement," "disinterested," "standards." The fifth sentence is the apex of both moral statement and rhetorical emphasis. Following two other balanced sentences, it heightens the sense of contrast by a pair of exactly matched constructions: "the glitter of their opportunities" and "the poverty of their achievement." The arrangement calls attention to the heaviest words in the passage, *opportunities* and *achievement*. But what do these words mean in the context? Surely they demand more of a wealthy society than that it be "picturesque." Behind *opportunities* we hear the echo of a moral order associated with traditional aristocratic groups—responsibilities of class, aesthetic and intellectual cultivation, standards of behavior accumulated from long experience in a privileged position. The abstract nouns are not generalizations drawn from Lily's society; they represent categories lifted from another social background and imposed on New York. The disparity stands out even more clearly when Gus Trenor checks himself after trying to make Lily "pay up" for the money he has given her: "Old habits, old restraints, the hand of inherited order, plucked back the bewildered mind which passion had jolted from its ruts" (p. 237). Here, as in much eighteenth-century writing, we find abstract nouns as subjects and verbs that animate the abstractions. But again the nouns arise from another social world than that portrayed in the novel. The "hand of inherited order" does not significantly guide Gus Trenor's circle of friends. To refer to "old habits, old restraints" is to create expectations about New York which that society simply cannot satisfy. The diction has a categorical firmness suggesting a solid and accepted moral order, but that order has no embodiment in the fictional world. The elevated and abstract language makes us confront the actions in the novel on a plane of moral refinement beyond the awareness of the characters themselves.

Such disparities between language and situation lead naturally to irony. The abstractions encourage us to look for much more than the concrete instance gives. Often the effect is comic, as in this summary of Percy Gryce: "Every form of prudence and suspicion had been grafted on a nature originally reluctant and cautious, with the result that it would have seemed hardly needful for Mrs. Gryce to extract his promise about the overshoes, so little likely was he to hazard himself abroad in the rain" (p. 34). But when Wharton analyzes Lily's situation, the irony becomes far less comic. Lily learns that the dullest of Mrs. Van Osburgh's daughters is engaged to Percy Gryce, whom she herself had hoped to marry:

Ah, lucky girls who grow up in the shelter of a mother's love—a mother who knows how to contrive opportunities without conceding favours, how to take advantage of propinquity without allowing appetite to be dulled by habit! The cleverest girl may miscalculate where her own interests are concerned, may yield too much at one moment and withdraw too far at the next: it takes a mother's unerring vigilance and foresight to land her daughters safely in the arms of wealth and suitability. [p. 146]

Wharton asks us to consider Lily's predicament in a framework of weighty abstractions. The language with its implied moral concepts echoes Jane Austen. But in the famous opening of *Pride and Prejudice*—"It is a truth universally acknowledged, that a single man in possession of a good fortune, must be in want of a wife"— we feel more security and control. This truth is *not* universally acknowledged, and the characters who think it is will be put in their places both by the author and by the society she portrays. The irony rests on assumed agreement about decorum among author, reader, and a right-minded social order.[2] In Wharton's passage this agreement is implied in the language, but it does not really exist. Presumably the calculated tactics of New York's mothers deviate from Wharton's norms for courtship, but within their society such mothers as Mrs. Van Osburgh help their daughters

---

[2]For a full discussion of how Jane Austen's style reflects such assumed agreement, see Howard S. Babb's fine study *Jane Austen's Novels: The Fabric of Dialogue* (Columbus, Ohio, 1962).

to succeed while Lily fails. The decorum, amiability, and rational propriety that ultimately prevail in Jane Austen's fictional world are not to be found in Edith Wharton's New York. Who in *The House of Mirth* represents "the arms of wealth and suitability"?

The author implied by Wharton's language bears much the same relationship to Lily as does Lawrence Selden. Both criticize Lily's society but neither offers her a better alternative within her powers. The language proposes norms for judgment that are nowhere realized in Lily's world. In other words, Wharton's irony does not single out deviant characters and lash them back into decorous conduct; rather it expresses her bitter judgment of a whole social order to which her ethical norms seem virtually irrelevant. Lily inhabits a world in which words like *suitability* have lost their meaning.

The distance between language and situation diminishes gradually from *The House of Mirth* (1905) to *The Age of Innocence* (1920). Several features contribute to the change, the most conspicuous being Wharton's increasing tendency to focus attention on the way the characters themselves use words:

"Now that things are comfortably settled—" [Amherst] knew so well what that elastic epithet covered![3]

Undine sat between Mr. Bowen and young Marvell, who struck her as very "sweet" (it was her word for friendliness). . . . [*Custom*, p. 34]

[Ralph] recalled all the old family catchwords, the full and elaborate vocabulary of evasion: "delicacy," "pride," "personal dignity," "preferring not to know about such things". . . . [*Custom*, p. 436]

Quotation marks repeatedly emphasize the socially accepted terminology, and frequently, as in these examples, Wharton adds direct analysis of such language. When she contrasts the still-viable category "friendliness" with "sweet," her conservatism in language points toward the more comprehensible, but by dismissing several other moral abstractions as "the vocabulary of evasion," she shows her growing awareness that the rhetoric of tradition must be carefully scrutinized in its application to current behavior.

Her scrutiny begins with a change in narrative technique between *The House of Mirth* and *The Custom of the Country*. Instead of

---

[3]*The Fruit of the Tree*, p. 178.

analyzing the issues in concise passages of ponderous Latinate phrasing, she moves in closer to the perceptions of her characters, imitating their various idioms and letting them talk more for themselves. She often interprets events through the viewpoints of characters within the novel, a procedure which makes the narrative more sprawling but which also gives the analytical language a double role: it probes social activities, and it determines the levels on which the characters themselves make their distinctions. Mrs. Heeny, the masseuse in *The Custom of the Country,* knows from professional experience the dullness of "cases" like Mrs. Spragg, stranded in New York with no friends or activities, but her language for more general social analysis comes from the clippings of *Town Talk:*

"If they don't know me they ain't in it."

"Mrs. Fairford gives the smartest little dinners in town."

"The wrong set's like fly-paper."

"And if young Marvell's taken with her she'll have the run of the place in no time."

Several other characters, including Undine, think in this same terminology: the substantive categories in this book emphasize social rather than moral discrimination. Whereas in *The House of Mirth* the "Oriental indolence and disorder" of the newcomers is measured against the "ordered activities," "inherited obligations," and "traditional functions" of the older families, in *The Custom of the Country* the distinction is between the "swells" and the "dowdy."

If most of the characters in this novel distinguish actions on the basis of what is or is not "in it," at least two retain a larger perspective. Ralph Marvell introduces and utilizes the concepts of anthropology—the "invaders" and the "aborigines." An even more detached onlooker is Charles Bowen, whose only function is to view the scene "impartially from the heights of pure speculation" (p. 205). He knows that the vocabulary of social discrimination forces people to take sides, and he prefers to seek general understanding. He analyzes "the custom of the country" less as a moralist than as a sociologist. Whereas Mrs. Ansell in *The Fruit of the Tree* categorizes the phenomenon abstractly—"the plan of bringing up our girls in the double bondage of expediency and unreality, corrupting their bodies with luxury and their brains with sentiment"[4]—Bowen tries to understand the system as it actually operates:

"The real paradox is the fact that the men who make, materially, the biggest sacrifices for their women, should do least for them ideally and romantically. And what's the result—how do the women avenge themselves? All my sympathy's with them, poor deluded dears, when I see their fallacious little attempts to trick out the leavings tossed them by the preoccupied male—the money and the motors and the clothes—and pretend to themselves and each other that *that's* what really constitutes life!" [p. 208]

The radical difference in style and diction here arises from the fact that Mrs. Ansell is giving the system a name, placing it morally; Bowen is explaining how it works. He avoids categories such as "expediency" and "luxury," which judge before they elucidate, and he qualifies his one moral substantive, "sacrifices," by "materially." For Bowen, actions take place among human beings rather than among moral abstractions, and these actions are motivated by human instincts, such as compensation and revenge.

Bowen reflects an important change in Wharton's thinking, a movement away from lofty moralizing and toward a prose style that explains processes or shows how her characters themselves make judgments. In *The Age of Innocence* she uses more concrete detail and analyzes it in less conceptual language: "But then New York, as far back as the mind of man could travel, had been divided into the two great fundamental groups of the Mingotts and Mansons and all their clan, who cared about eating and clothes and money, and the Archer-Newland-van-der-Luyden tribe, who were devoted to travel, horticulture and the best fiction, and looked down on the grosser forms of pleasure" (pp. 30-31). Instead of "Oriental indolence and disorder" and "inherited obligations," or the "swells" and the "dowdy," we have simply "two great fundamental groups." Although the epithets urbanely satirize New York's provincialism, the abstraction itself is ethically and socially neutral; it prepares us for a distinction based not on names but on relatively specific description. Such a sentence tries to make some

---

[4]Ibid., p. 281.

sense of New York's manners rather than summarily judge them. I will return to this development in discussing syntax, but first I want to examine another implication of Wharton's earlier categorical language.

Pointed Constructions and the Epigram

When generic language imposes moral categories that elevate the situation more than seems appropriate, the abstract and the specific can be brought together in striking, pointed constructions. The surface of Wharton's early fiction sparkles with ironic turns of thought and phrase, epigrams, and sudden, sharp generalizations.[5]

Genius is of small use to a woman who does not know how to do her hair.[6]

Lily reviewed them with a scornful impatience: . . . young Silverton, who had meant to live on proof-reading and write an epic, and who now lived on his friends and had become critical of truffles; Alice Wetherall, an animated visiting-list, whose most fervid convictions turned on the wording of invitations and the engraving of dinner-cards; . . . Gwen Van Osburgh, with all the guileless confidence of a young girl who has always been told that there is no one richer than her father. [*House*, pp. 87-88]

She was realizing for the first time that a woman's dignity may cost more to keep up than her carriage. . . . [*House*, p. 273]

It was not, after all, opportunity but imagination that he lacked: he had a mental palate which would never learn to distinguish between railway tea and nectar. [*House*, p. 30]

To attempt to bring her into active relation with life was like tugging at a piece of furniture which has been screwed to the floor. [*House*, p. 59]

Such pithy statements can be lifted out of context without much loss. Whether they summarize a social development, a character, or a general truth about human experience, they involve the same basic working of the mind: presenting a moral phrase or an ab-

---

[5]Each of the following critics comments on the epigram as a hallmark of Edith Wharton's style: E. K. Brown, *Edith Wharton: Étude Critique* (Paris, 1935), esp. the chapter "Le Style"; Viola Hopkins [Winner], "The Ordering Style of *The Age of Innocence*," *American Literature*, 30 (1958), 345-57; Irving Howe, Introduction, *The House of Mirth* (New York, 1962).

[6]*The Touchstone* (New York, 1900), p. 15.

stract generalization and following it up with a particularity. What is significant about these constructions is that the judgment precedes the specific description. They deliver opinion rather than develop argument, and they have an effect of finality. The feeling of certitude in such phrasing implies that particular actions are being measured against absolute laws.

By emphasizing condensed moralistic summaries, Wharton's style suggests her temperamental affiliations with Stoicism. In his studies of seventeenth-century prose style, Morris Croll points to aphorisms, *sententiae*, and golden sayings as the formal ideal of Stoic style.[7] Stoicism seeks universal laws through the jostling appearances and turns of fortune that are bound up with social conventions alien to the soul. When such laws are discovered, they impose their truth immediately and forcefully on the thinker. But because this truth is moral and inward, it does not fit the rhetoric of orators, who must appeal by schemes of words and sounds to the feelings of the multitude. Instead Stoicism favors forms of expression involving figures of wit, and since it flourishes when the best ideas are at odds with a corrupting society, Stoicism often clothes its penetrating insights in significant brevity and obscurity, mocking orthodoxy while affirming natural law. As Stoic philosophy asks man to accommodate himself to universal law, so Wharton's pointed constructions demand our immediate agreement and castigate a social order that disregards the moral ideals she upholds. The flash of insight, the sharp ironic turn from lofty morality to immediate frivolity, tends to surprise and overwhelm the reader just as the discovery of law and truth behind confusing appearances overpowers the Stoic moralist and forces his unqualified assent. And the distance between law and appearance in Wharton's phrasing corresponds exactly to the distance I described in the Introduction between moral expectancies and social observations.

By asserting final judgment and suggesting universal law, Wharton's epigrams reinforce her abstract diction. As her early language shows her trying to give names to the actions in the

---

[7]See the essays "'Attic Prose' in the Seventeenth Century," "Attic Prose: Lipsius, Montaigne, Bacon," and "The Baroque Style in Prose," in Morris W. Croll, *Style, Rhetoric, and Rhythm*, ed. J. Max Patrick (Princeton, 1966).

fiction, to place them in moral categories, so the aphoristic phrasing reveals her desire to reduce processes to their underlying conceptual form, to condense historical and social development into a penetrating generalized statement. In chapter 1 I discussed Wharton's ideas about history and referred to Odo Valsecca's excitement at making intellectual sense of social change: "His imagination, taking the intervening obstacles at a bound, arrived at once at the general axiom to which such inductions pointed; . . . he afterward learned that human development follows no such direct line of advance, but must painfully stumble across the wastes of error, prejudice and ignorance, while the theorizer traverses the same distance with a stroke of his speculative pinions."[8]

Let us now consider this passage as a statement about intellectual and literary style. What are Wharton's aphorisms but strokes of her "speculative pinions," condensed "general axioms" that overleap particularities and satisfy the imaginative desire for general truth? Even as she recognizes the "intervening obstacles," she dismisses them in a lofty categorical phrase—real human development stumbles "across the wastes of error, prejudice and ignorance." Throughout her historical novel *The Valley of Decision*, she seeks fundamental concepts of social change, introducing her specific scenes with abstract summaries.

Only later does Wharton account specifically and at length for that stumbling across the wastes of error that characterizes real human development. In 1928 she described in retrospect her own change in style, telling how early critics had praised her "brilliancy": "Experience, however, subdued my natural tendency to 'put things' pointedly, and I became conscious—and happily conscious—of having reduced my style to a more even and unnoticeable texture."[9] This smoothing down of the prose texture involves a corresponding shift in her way of conceptualizing experience, a greater willingness to analyze and describe, not simply to sum up. The harsh distinction between authorial phrasing and social reality is softened by her greater attention to the perceptions of

---

[8] *Valley*, I, 260.

[9] Edith Wharton, "A Cycle of Reviewing," *Spectator* (London), 141 (3 Nov. 1928), 45.

her characters, and the significantly brief epigram is spread out into longer, more analytical constructions.

In *The Age of Innocence* the epigrammatic structure has been expanded from the phrase or sentence to such paragraphs as the following:

> It was thus, Archer reflected, that New York managed its transitions: conspiring to ignore them till they were well over, and then, in all good faith, imagining that they had taken place in a preceding age. There was always a traitor in the citadel; and after he (or generally she) had surrendered the keys, what was the use of pretending that it was impregnable? Once people had tasted of Mrs. Struthers's easy Sunday hospitality they were not likely to sit at home remembering that her champagne was transmuted Shoe-Polish. [p. 262]

Here the basic statement is made in three ways: first in a clear general statement, next in a metaphor, and finally in the particular instance. Wharton moves gradually from her own abstractions to the mental range of most New Yorkers, tempering her irony by a smoother, more analytical progression. And the generalization itself is not a law of human experience by which we evaluate the specific detail; instead it tells abstractly what is going on in this particular society. The distance between general and particular has diminished.

In spite of these important changes in style, certain features associated with the epigram survive in Wharton's prose. She continues to move, often ironically, from the general to the specific, from her own perceptions to those of her characters, and this progression influences our judgment of manners in the fiction. By beginning with rational, abstract phrasing, she makes us entertain moral ideas while she goes on to particular details, recounting customary behavior. Thus we demand moral significance as we learn about manners. When the demands are too great for the manners presented, as often happens in *The House of Mirth*, the manners themselves seem corrupt. But when the generalization asks only slightly more from the manners than they offer, the structure gives intellectual density to seemingly arbitrary codes of behavior, making manners both comprehensible and worthy of comprehension. It is this happy compromise that characterizes the style of *The Age of Innocence*.

Syntax: the Texture of Judgment

In narrative prose marked by pointed constructions and imposing diction, one tends to neglect the stylistic base against which the conspicuous phrasing is defined. But it is through her more general habits of syntax that Wharton's prose style works its profoundest effects, and these habits are most evident in *The Age of Innocence*, where her development of a smooth, tight, analytical prose reached its peak. Some of the peculiar qualities of her syntax can be ascertained by a random glance at sentences that open chapters:

On a January evening of the early seventies, Christine Nilsson was singing in *Faust* at the Academy of Music in New York. [p. 1]

In the course of the next day the first of the usual betrothal visits were exchanged. [p. 24]

Some two weeks later, Newland Archer, sitting in abstracted idleness in his private compartment of the office of Letterblair, Lamson and Low, attorneys at law, was summoned by the head of the firm. [p. 90]

Every year on the fifteenth of October Fifth Avenue opened its shutters, unrolled its carpets and hung up its triple layer of window-curtains. [p. 258]

Newland Archer sat at the writing-table in his library in East Thirty-ninth Street. [p. 347]

These sentences, short, definite, and grammatically simple, place us immediately in the middle, not of an action, but of a situation. Wharton often begins her chapters and her long paragraphs of analysis with such brief statements, subsequently exploring the complexities behind them. In spite of their relatively simple syntax, however, these sentences are stylistically informative. They depend heavily on prepositional phrases, which expand the subject and predicate by an account of time, place, and circumstance. Wharton seems more' concerned with the relations of ideas, people, actions, or objects to their surroundings than with the attributes of things in themselves. Her sentences immerse us in a well-defined social world: things are in their places; actions have an accorded time; individuals fit into a larger pattern. The second example, particularly, illustrates a social activity proceeding independently of its participants. The passive verb is suspended until the end of the sentence, allowing the ordered elements of the ritual to precede the action.

Many of her sentences are, of course, considerably more complex:

The Beauforts' house was one of the few in New York that possessed a ball-room (it antedated even Mrs. Manson Mingott's and the Headly Chiverses); and at a time when it was beginning to be thought "provincial" to put a "crash" over the drawing-room floor and move the furniture upstairs, the possession of a ballroom that was used for no other purpose, and left for three-hundred-and-sixty-four days of the year to shuttered darkness, with its gilt chairs stacked in a corner and its chandelier in a bag; this undoubted superiority was felt to compensate for whatever was regrettable in the Beaufort past. [p. 16]

In this long construction there are only two independent or main clauses, one of the verbs being the copulative *was*, and the other a passive, *was felt*. Subordinate clauses and prepositional phrases expand the sentence, not by qualifying an action but by elaborating a mental state of affairs. Many details about entertaining in the seventies emerge from the sentence, but they are embedded in complicated grammatical structures that establish firm conceptual relationships among them. In the second main clause so much material is included in the subject ("the possession . . . in a bag") that Wharton has to add a demonstrative pronoun to carry on the sense of her sentence. The phrase "this undoubted superiority" summarizes everything that has preceded it and expresses New York's judgment of the Beaufort ballroom. Such summary phrases appear throughout the novel, compressing an accumulation of detail and explanation into a moralistic category that reflects the thinking of New Yorkers. Of course, these phrases are usually ironic—conspicuous material waste does not constitute "superiority"—but they reveal with precision the way in which particular manners enter into society's moral evaluation.

Wharton conveys the judgments of old New York in several other ways as well. The parenthetical construction illustrates New York's tendency to make careful comparisons, and the adverb *even* refines the evaluation. There is an abundance of adverbial modification in the novel, most of it suggesting the fastidious appraisals of New York. Viola Hopkins Winner has pointed out that the frequent parentheses and quotation marks in this novel are devices to project the voice and accepted attitudes of the society.[10] Wharton's syntax emphasizes this effect. She favors sentence patterns that allow her to enclose direct actions or facts in larger constructions that judge them and discriminate among them: "it was beginning to be thought '*provincial*' to put a 'crash' over the drawing-room floor and move the furniture upstairs." Simple statements describing social behavior are transformed into dependent structures—subordinate clauses, prepositional, infinitive, or participial phrases—and inserted as specifiers of the abstract judgments. By this procedure Wharton forces us to entertain the actions indirectly and tentatively, on a plane of refined discrimination; we contemplate and judge manners rather than simply observe them. That is, as we proceed through a sentence, instead of asking, What are we to think of putting a "crash" on the floor? we ask, What is provincial? Thus particular manners are encased in syntactic frames that evaluate them by New York's standards. And in this example the judgment-insert construction is itself contained in a subordinate clause. The details of social behavior are tightly subordinated to the main clause, which expresses the relationships between moral abstractions: "this undoubted superiority was felt to compensate for whatever was regrettable in the Beaufort past."

If such syntactic patterns convey precisely the way New York discriminates and qualifies manners, what effect does this syntax have on Wharton's drawing of the inner life? The following paragraph presents Newland Archer's reflections after three months of marriage:

Archer had reverted to all his old inherited ideas about marriage. It was less trouble to conform with the tradition and treat May exactly as all his friends treated their wives than to try to put into practice the theories with which his untrammelled bachelorhood had dallied. There was no use in trying to emancipate a wife who had not the dimmest notion that she was not free; and he had long since discovered that May's only use of the liberty she supposed herself to possess would be to lay it on the altar of her wifely adoration. Her innate dignity would always keep her from making the gift abjectly; and a day might even come (as it once had) when she would find strength to take it altogether back if she thought she were doing it for his own good. But with

[10]Viola Hopkins [Winner], p. 351. This article describes Wharton's creation of a double vision—her own and society's—by using serious words for trivialities and moralistic words for conventions.

a conception of marriage so uncomplicated and incurious as hers such a crisis could be brought about only by something visibly outrageous in his own conduct; and the fineness of her feeling for him made that unthinkable. Whatever happened, he knew, she would always be loyal, gallant and unresentful; and that pledged him to the practice of the same virtues. [pp. 196-97]

Again direct actions are subordinated to refined discriminations. In the second, third, and fourth sentences the main clauses express judgments or qualifications of particular manners:

It was less trouble—INSERT—than—INSERT.

There was no use—INSERT.

Her innate dignity would always keep her—INSERT.

And in the third and fourth sentences two subordinate clauses indicate refined perceptions about possible actions or states of being:

who had not the dimmest notion—INSERT

when she would find strength—INSERT

The following sentences have all been nominalized, grammatically transformed into dependent structures and embedded as specifiers of the judgments and qualifications in the positions indicated:

Archer conformed with the tradition and treated May exactly as all his friends treated their wives.
Archer tried to put into practice the theories with which his untrammelled bachelorhood had dallied.
Archer tried to emancipate a wife who had not the dimmest notion that she was not free.
She made the gift abjectly.
She was not free.
She would take it altogether back if she thought she were doing it for his own good.

Each of these embedded statements designates a direct action or a simple fact, but in the larger construction the action becomes tentative, a subject for speculation, comparison, and evaluation. And by the time we reach the actions themselves, the judgments have already been made.

The sense of elaborate appraisal is heightened by the cluster of adverbial modifiers and qualifying determiners: *all, exactly, long since, only, always, abjectly, altogether, so . . . as . . ., such, visibly.*

There is also a parenthetical construction that functions adverbially and a clause introduced by an adverb of comparison: "exactly as all his friends treated their wives." The prose style reflects a mind constantly bent on discerning and assessing fine shades of behavior. Frequently in the novel that mind represents the collective arbiter "New York," but here the mind is Archer's, and his own scrupulous judgment of his marriage reflects the influence of New York thought on his inner life.

If Archer's qualifications echo those of New York, the syntax of the last three sentences shows New York's obligations to be active agents in the moral life. May's "innate dignity" is less an individual characteristic than the product of a firm tradition, and this abstraction is the subject of the fourth sentence; it causes May to preserve decorum in submitting to her husband and makes her constantly evaluate his worthiness of that submission. The fifth sentence begins with a lengthy absolute construction: "with a conception of marriage so uncomplicated and incurious as hers." The stylistic effect of this locution appears immediately if we compare it with such an alternative as "her conception of marriage being so uncomplicated and incurious." Wharton's choice illustrates her tendency to transform the immediate into a more general moral statement. The logic of the fifth sentence applies not only to May and Archer but to any marriage in which the husband and wife are products of New York traditions. The first main clause is passive, the agent being a moral quality defined by New York's standards, "something visibly outrageous in his own conduct." In the second clause the subject is again an abstract quality, "the fineness of her feeling for him."

Not only are moral abstractions the active agents, but the cross-references in these sentences bind together a whole system of obligations. In the fourth sentence "the gift" and "it" refer back to the preceding sentence; "such a crisis" summarizes the conjecture of the fourth sentence; "that" in the fifth sentence refers to the possibility of outrageous conduct; and "that" in the sixth sentence turns May's virtues into an abstract agent forcing Archer to behave with similar decorum. Each clause is linked to the preceding in a tight web of responsibilities.

Thus Wharton's syntax conveys the strength of New York's manners as they affect a refined sensibility. The first half of the paragraph presents, in a highly tentative form, Archer's thoughts of larger possibilities for himself and his wife, but the subtle logic in the remainder of the paragraph illustrates how conventions have become a tenuous yet powerful ethical system forcing Archer to revert "to all his old inherited ideas." Archer's mind is far from independent; society's limitations are ingrained in the very way he thinks. The whole paragraph is presented on an abstract plane, but the moral categories fall within Archer's comprehension, demanding no more of his conduct than is possible within the confines of his society. The subordinate clauses, dependent phrases, and prepositional phrases place each part of the paragraph in well-established relationships to the other parts, defining a complex, dignified, but ultimately restrictive system.

Although appropriate to its subject, such a syntactic web is by no means inevitable for a novelist who emphasizes abstract qualities and nuances of behavior. The following two passages throw into relief the peculiarities of Wharton's style. Each presents a situation roughly similar to that in the example above—a character of fine sensibility and idealistic yearnings is trying to understand the feelings of disillusionment and entrapment following marriage to a meaner nature. The two characters are Dorothea Brooke in George Eliot's *Middlemarch* and Isabel Archer in Henry James's *The Portrait of a Lady.*

How was it that in the weeks since her marriage, Dorothea had not distinctly observed but felt with a stifling depression, that the large vistas and wide fresh air which she had dreamed of finding in her husband's mind were replaced by anterooms and winding passages which seemed to lead nowhither? I suppose it was that in courtship everything is regarded as provisional and preliminary, and the smallest sample of virtue or accomplishment is taken to guarantee delightful stores which the broad leisure of marriage will reveal. But the door-sill of marriage once crossed, expectation is concentrated on the present. Having once embarked on your marital voyage, it is impossible not to be aware that you make no way and that the sea is not within sight—that, in fact, you are exploring an enclosed basin. . . . Her husband's way of commenting on the strangely impressive objects around them had begun to affect her with a sort of mental shiver: he had perhaps the best intention of acquitting himself worthily, but only of acquitting himself. What was fresh to her mind was worn out to his.[11]

---

[11]*Middlemarch* (Boston, 1956), pp. 145-46.

This mistrust was now the clearest result of their short married life; a gulf had opened between them over which they looked at each other with eyes that were on either side a declaration of the deception suffered. It was a strange opposition, of the like of which she had never dreamed—an opposition in which the vital principle of the one was a thing of contempt to the other. It was not her fault—she had practised no deception; she had only admired and believed. She had taken all the first steps in the purest confidence, and then she had suddenly found the infinite vista of a multiplied life to be a dark, narrow alley with a dead wall at the end. Instead of leading to the high places of happiness, from which the world would seem to lie below one, so that one could look down with a sense of exaltation and advantage, and judge and choose and pity, it led rather downward and earthward, into realms of restriction and depression where the sound of other lives, easier and freer, was heard as from above, and where it served to deepen the feeling of failure.[12]

Both authors depend considerably more on imagery than Wharton. The "vista" expresses all those possibilities of ardent action and expanded consciousness that characterize the ideals of Dorothea and Isabel. In defining the way in which expectation has been defeated, the imagery brings into play powerful feelings and suggests broad imaginative ramifications. The disillusionments of Dorothea and Isabel move us more deeply than Archer's because they seem to include more. By appealing more purely to the intellect, Wharton's modes of expression limit both desire and loss. Instead of imagining multiplied vistas, Archer has "dallied" with "theories." Wharton does use imagery, but not as a unifying mode of thought. Her metaphors clarify immediate issues rather than suggest the subtle imaginative changes occurring slowly and continuously throughout a novel. In referring to the "pyramid" of New York society, its "tribal rites," the "Gorgon" of experience, and May's "Diana-like aloofness," Wharton sharpens the mental picture of a specific social or moral situation, but she does not engage the imagination or imply changes of feeling in the shifting of a given image.

The prose styles of George Eliot and Henry James encourage freer expansion than Wharton's. In *Middlemarch* the authorial voice intrudes often and easily with generalizations, but these comments do not have Wharton's categorical finality. They place

[12]*Portrait*, II, 189.

the characters' immediate problems in the large context of human experience; the expectations of courtship do not single out Dorothea herself or the rural society of nineteenth-century England, but appeal instead to what all sympathetic readers can share imaginatively. Dorothea is falling into human experience, not into a specific social complex; her situation is at once broader and more personal than Archer's. James's style is even more expansive. The clauses and phrases in the quoted passage are only loosely tied together, often as appositives, each of them reaching out in a new direction, suggesting many possible ramifications of Isabel's situation. The larger blocks of James's analytical prose are made coherent less by tight syntactical connections than by unifying imagery. The last sentence in the example shows a mind responding subtly to the various shades of "it"—"the infinite vista of a multiplied life." James often suspends such pronouns over long passages, emphasizing the multiplied complexity of the feelings and implications associated with a given image or idea. Wharton, on the other hand, compresses and limits preceding ideas into summary phrases, such as "this undoubted superiority." Her logic is more self-contained, just as her syntax forms a tighter web of thought. Because she uses intellectual and moral abstractions rather than images, she must seek coherence in firm grammatical connections, enclosing subtleties in precise subordinate positions.

Whereas both George Eliot and Henry James refer their styles simultaneously to nuances of conduct and subtleties of feeling, Wharton explores more purely the subtleties of conduct and obligation. George Eliot's style is particularly suited to defining the expectations and the ardent personal feelings which are defeated. She moves into the hearts of each of her characters, where a variety of feelings jostle against, and replace, each other; from this perspective all the other characters seem curiously alien. James's style is calculated to define the subtle relationships between individuals. Wharton's style develops neither ardent personal ideals nor complex relationships between well-defined individual characters. The peculiar genius of her prose lies in its defining the traditions, duties, and social assumptions that impede the individual. As her syntax embeds particularities of behavior in a framework of firm judgment, her fiction itself encloses individual desires in a well-ordered network of social obligations.

In diction, turn of phrase, and syntax, Wharton's style appeals to the intellect and the moral sense, but she neglects the imagination and seems to distrust the feelings. Her virtues are clarity, precision, dignity, and astute judgment. She conveys delicate nuances of behavior, but her subtleties express the complexity of the social order rather than the imaginative range of the individual mind. We must go to James for the expanding possibilities of the human spirit; Wharton describes what limits it.

Chapter VI

The Ritualistic Social Scene
An Assessment

SINCE MANNERS ARE those gestures that have social significance, they appear most extensively at formal gatherings. Consequently, the novel of manners employs as characteristic scenes such public assemblies as dinners, evenings at the opera or theater, balls, and receptions. In such scenes the novelist reveals the importance of manners in his fictional world. Not only can he bring together several characters with conflicting personal interests, but he can show how social conventions relate these characters to each other, setting up patterns of behavior and propriety that control individual expression. With several characters scrutinizing and judging each other, responding as much to the overtones of conventional gestures as to the direct meaning of a character's words, such scenes have a peculiar intensity. Individual feelings play against the habits and expectations of a whole social order.

Through his handling of these formal scenes, a novelist illustrates his attitudes toward manners and society. When Stendhal's Julien Sorel, for example, attends his first formal dinner in the Hôtel de la Mole, he wears boots instead of the low shoes proper to a secretary, and he steps on the marquis's toe in entering the dining room, but he impresses the guests and amuses the host with his knowledge of the classics. Speaking seriously and originally, he cuts through the Parisian language of wit with its ready-made judgments and epigrams. That is, he succeeds socially *despite*, not through, the conventions of Paris. Throughout *The Red and the Black* Stendhal opposes the spontaneous and the calculated, using dinner and opera scenes rather to satirize the boredom and fixity of Parisian manners than to show these manners constraining his hero. In *Père Goriot* Balzac seems to feel that the formal assembly stifles the expression of those sublime passions and noble sentiments that can elevate his characters. When the Viscountess de Beauséant is forsaken by her lover, she gives a ball before retiring from Parisian society. Many persons gather to witness her defeat, some with gratified malice and others with pitying curiosity, but Balzac treats the public scene only briefly and generally, saying that the viscountess maintained poise and a controlled smile. He must move her away from the formal gathering to the privacy of her bedroom in order to dramatize the grief and noble repression that educate his protagonist, young Rastignac. Being concerned with the laws of the human heart, Balzac finds the formal scene too limiting to be more than a spectacle of self-control before an audience. He shows the malice underlying polite manners, but his significant actions take place in circumstances less constrained by codified forms of behavior and thus more susceptible to the shaping force of personal passion.

Unlike Balzac and Stendhal, Edith Wharton finds formal gatherings so congenial to her narrative interests that they epitomize her work as a novelist. Not only does she use such scenes extensively, but she encloses critical actions and revelations in them. The first five chapters of *The Age of Innocence*, for example, present a series of formal scenes—the opera, the Beaufort ball, the first betrothal visit, and Mrs. Archer's dinner for Sillerton Jackson. In these scenes Archer meets Ellen Olenska, becomes engaged to May, commits himself to defending the countess's reputation, and finds himself beginning to question New York's values. Indeed it is in the social scene, so formalized as to become a ritual, that Wharton realizes her finest narrative art. In such scenes she consolidates and dramatizes the subject of her paramount concern—the working power of a set of manners.

Wharton's handling of formal scenes is distinctive in a number of ways. She is too concerned with the full dynamics of a social order to foreshorten such scenes, as do Stendhal and Balzac, in the interest of special emphases. And she takes public pressure too seriously to stylize it. Rather than reduce the complexity of maneuver in a public gathering, she registers here the operative values of a society, revealing the conventions through which it facilitates its activities and analyzing the means by which it integrates separate personalities. Such social powers obviously restrict the individual, but Wharton also sees in them an adjustment to human needs, as is apparent in her depiction of Mrs. Fairford's dinner near the outset of *The Custom of the Country*. It is Undine Spragg's first formal dinner in New York, and her anticipations set off the qualities of the scene. She expects lavish gilding, a smart new artificial fire, elaborate culinary innovation, and brilliant talk about people. She is bewildered to find herself in a world of half-tones. The fire is real; the meat dishes are substantial but simple; and the quiet talk turns on general topics. Mrs. Fairford exemplifies the traditions and values of Washington Square: pleasure in sub-dued and restful surroundings, concern for the comfort and enjoyment of her guests. Conversation to her is a "concert" rather than a "solo"; she draws out each of her guests, fitting them into an overall pattern, and as Undine perceives this pattern, she tempers her own desire to dominate the scene. Although she is disappointed in the dinner and the guests, she is sufficiently imita-tive to accommodate herself to the "spirit of caution" that prevails. And when Undine later regains her personal confidence and increasingly asserts her own desires against the pattern of such gatherings, it is clear that we are witnessing, not the triumph of honesty over artificiality, but the destruction of a social order.

The assumptions underlying Wharton's presentation of this dinner stand in sharp contrast to those more common in the novel of manners. In the opening chapter of *War and Peace*, for example, Tolstoy compares Anna Pávlovna, the hostess at the soiree, to the foreman of a spinning mill, seeing that each spindle in the "con-versational machine" turns steadily and without excessive noise.[1] When Pierre Bezúkhov takes ideas seriously and, worse yet, becomes enthusiastic about theories, Anna Pávlovna steers him into the larger circle and changes the subject of conversation. Tolstoy sees the forms of social behavior as designed to keep seriousness and enthusiasm at a minimum; comfort takes prece-dence over honesty, and when the foolish Prince Hippolyte diverts attention from an argument about Napoleon by an absurd and dull story, most of the guests are relieved. Where Wharton emphasizes those aspects of manners that draw out and integrate individuals, Tolstoy stresses manners that restrain intellectual ardor. Of course,

---

[1]Although *War and Peace* can hardly be classified as a novel of manners, Tolstoy's concerns with history and historiography play against his presentation of human experi-ence in modes appropriate to the novel of manners. His peacetime narratives, especially those in St. Petersburg, illustrate those qualities that make Tolstoy one of Wharton's primary examples of a novelist of manners.

a significant difference between Tolstoy and Wharton is that his characters have more important things to think and talk about than hers.

Mrs. Fairford's dinner illustrates another reason for the importance of social gatherings in Wharton's fiction; the contrast of social values emerges with precision. And if such scenes can mark in detail the distinctions between social orders, they provide an even more exact measure of an individual's deviations from his own class. Against the backdrop of conventional expectations, characters can express their feelings and define their individuality by slight gestures and inflections, which suggest emotional force constrained by formal circumstances. Thus when Newland Archer decides during the last opera scene to tell May that he loves Madame Olenska, New York can take the full measure of his agitation, his neglect of social boundaries, by observing that he enters the van der Luyden box in the middle of a solo. New York's ritual of not even talking during a solo, much less moving about, gives more emotional resonance to Archer's dissatisfaction with himself and his society than Wharton could convey directly.

Finally, then, it is not simply their narrative potentialities that make social gatherings congenial to Wharton's fiction; they suit her predispositions about human feelings. When she creates scenes in which convention exerts its maximum pressure, she herself seems curiously freed to articulate the imaginative yearnings of a character trapped by his society. Aspiration and desire tend to dissolve in her fiction unless they are contained in society's ceremonial forms and revealed in muted gestures. Distrusting both the open expression of passion and the vague bliss of fulfillment, she prefers to suggest strong feelings under a restrained surface.

Beyond these specific functions in the narratives, however, Wharton's formal scenes create powerful images that consolidate the major tendencies of her fiction. She puts the self on stage and then conveys to the reader an extraordinary sense of the audience. Few other novelists suggest so forcefully the pressure of onlookers scrutinizing a character's actions. The picnic at Box Hill in *Emma* and the opera at Brussels in *Vanity Fair* approach Wharton's procedure in this respect. But Austen and Thackeray have individualized the witnesses; Emma and Becky perform before particular persons, who have their own idiosyncrasies, motives, and weaknesses. The society before which Wharton's characters act is less differentiated; Lily Bart, Undine Spragg, and Newland Archer perceive their audience as a compact and often formidable whole rather than as an assembly of individuals. When Archer recognizes in his dinner guests a conspiracy to separate himself from Ellen, the realization comes over him "in a vast flash made up of many broken gleams"; the glances and inflections of separate people merge into a unified force. Instead of intertwining several distinct relationships among characters gathered formally, Wharton shows her protagonists acting before an unspecified group; they are conscious primarily of being watched.

In this regard, no one approaches Edith Wharton's peculiar effects more closely than Nathaniel Hawthorne in the magnificent opening tableau of *The Scarlet Letter*—the self elevated before, and judged by, the community of witnesses. And perhaps it is in projecting the audience that Wharton reveals her deepest affiliation with her own countrymen; for the massing of an abstract public, set over against the individual, represents a major tendency of American fiction and of American manners as well. While describing the clubs of New York in *The American Scene*, Henry James develops one of his keenest observations about social habits and their outward forms. He notes in American buildings—public or private—only the vaguest boundaries between one place and another; every suggestion of the room-character is minimized by "the indefinite extension of all spaces." In eliminating outward exclusory arrangements for the sake of democratic openness, the American necessarily raises the pitch of social relations from intimate conversation to the shriek. The visitor, accustomed to localizing backgrounds, limits, and arrangements for privacy,

sees only doorless apertures, vainly festooned, which decline to tell him where he is, which make him still a homeless wanderer, which show him other apertures, corridors, staircases, yawning, expanding, ascending, descending, and all as for the purpose of giving his presence "away," of reminding him that what he says must be said for the house. He is beguiled in a measure by reading into these phenomena, ever so sharply, the reason of many another impression; he is beguiled by remembering how many of the things said in America *are* said for the house.[2]

---

[2]*The American Scene* (New York, 1907), pp. 162-63.

What James here sees so clearly about American manners Wharton works directly into her narrative methods. She paraphrases James's observations in the words of her own Europeanized American, Ellen Olenska, about the van der Luydens' house at Skuytercliff: " 'One can't be alone for a minute in that great seminary of a house, with all the doors wide open, and always a servant bringing tea, or a log for the fire, or the newspaper! Is there nowhere in an American house where one may be by one's self? You're so shy, and yet you're so public. I always feel as if I were in the convent again—or on the stage, before a dreadfully polite audience that never applauds' " (*Age*, pp. 131-32). Where James sees the possibility of an audience and a tendency for conversation to become oratory, Edith Wharton sees the audience itself as ever-present, forcing conversation to become the self-conscious enactment of a dramatic role. Undine Spragg regards social activity as a "performance," and she practices gestures and facial expressions before a mirror. As she watches others to learn new movements and tricks of phrase, she expects to be watched herself. And Newland Archer, alone with Ellen Olenska, finds himself wonderfully freed from "the sense of playing a part before sophisticated witnesses."

Wharton keeps us aware of the "witnesses" in several ways, the most obvious being a narrative intrusion. When Undine has her first private talk with Ralph, it is in an opera box, and Wharton reminds us in the middle of their dialogue that Mabel Lipscomb is also in the box but has discreetly turned away. After her engagement to Ralph has been announced, Undine's own consciousness of triumph at the theater conveys the presence of an audience; she feels herself the center of envious and curious glances. When she sees Clare Van Degen and Harriet Ray watching her, she lifts "a smile of possessorship" to Ralph. But alert surveillance also poses a threat. After Ralph leaves his seat to greet Clare and Harriet, Undine finds Elmer Moffatt on her other side and must speak to him, at least briefly. To emphasize the pressure of onlookers, Wharton shifts the point of view to the Van Degen box, where Clare asks Ralph who the red-faced man is talking to Miss Spragg. Similarly, after Newland Archer has himself participated in the club box's inspection of the Mingott box across the opera hall, he cannot escape his awareness that the eyes of "masculine New

York" are on him when he goes around to visit May and to meet Ellen.

Furthermore, the witnesses do not disappear when the scene shifts to less public surroundings. In Wharton's characteristically contrived narratives, if a private and possibly compromising action *can* be observed, it will be, and by exactly those persons who can put the worst construction on it. New York's surveillance is inexhaustible; its knowledge of private lives virtually complete. When Lily Bart leaves Selden's apartment, she encounters Simon Rosedale; when she escapes from Gus Trenor's house at night after resisting his sexual assault, she is seen by Selden. And while talking to Ellen on Fifth Avenue at night, Archer notices the approach of Lawrence Lefferts and a young Chivers, who emphasize their own assumptions by discreetly cutting across to the other side of the street.

Wharton also suggests the audience by phrases recounting a generalized response to the actions and words of her characters. During the dinner at which Undine meets Urban Dagonet, for example, her words about divorce fall on "a pause which prolonged and deepened itself to receive them, while every face at the table, Ralph Marvell's excepted, reflected in varying degree Mr. Dagonet's pained astonishment" (*Custom*, p. 94). Here the listeners emerge as a unified body, and the phrase "every face at the table" makes this body seem more extensive than it actually is.

When Wharton's characters attend the theater or the opera, the boundaries of the stage extend into the audience. As much goes on in the boxes and stalls as on the formal stage, and the audience's attention seems more keenly focused on the actions of society than on those of the hired performers. In the opening scene of *The Age of Innocence*, May Welland's blush is as precisely timed and conventional as the *"M'ama!"* sung by Madame Nilsson, and Archer responds to both with the same heightened pleasure. In fact, this entire scene is a ritual celebration in which the sexual undercurrents of the audience are objectified and contained in the ceremonial forms of the stage. As "the little brown Faust-Capoul" tries to seduce Gretchen–Madame Nilsson, who affects "a guileless incomprehension of his designs," the unmarried males of New York line up in the club box to scrutinize the innocent young girls opposite.

The metaphor of the theater underlies Wharton's formal scenes much as the metaphor of the game is integral to her scenes between two people. She frequently composes her characters in pictorial scenes—in the *tableaux vivants* of Mrs. Wellington Bry's entertainments, on the lawns at Bellomont and Newport, about a dinner table, or in theater boxes—but these groupings are more than simply studies of the static relationships within society. Occurring repeatedly at moments when private lines of narrative development reach a crisis in public, such compositions set the stage for important choices. Constrained by codes of accepted behavior, watched by an alert and ever-present audience, Wharton's characters must commit themselves to serious actions. They are on stage, and they know the conventional mannerisms for various roles, but they must improvise the parts they play, and each role they choose diminishes their range of choice in subsequent scenes.

Two of the finest scenes in *The House of Mirth* occur under these theatrical circumstances. In chapter 3 I discussed Lily's appeasement of Rosedale at the wedding reception, showing how the pressure of being watched forces her to accept his intimacy. Even more impressive is the scene in which Bertha Dorset cuts Lily. The scene occurs at the end of a lavish dinner party given by the Wellington Brys. The social issues of inclusion and exclusion are especially tense in this party because of the Brys' underlying purpose. By bringing together and amusing a select group of European aristocrats and the Dorsets, who hold the keys to New York's social citadel, they hope to penetrate New York society. During the dinner, which is seen through Selden's eyes, Lily demonstrates the grace and discrimination that show her as an exquisite product of her society and at the same time detach her from that society by her very fineness. Among the guests Wharton adroitly includes "little Dabham" of the "Riviera Notes," alive to intimations about who stands where in society and prepared to immortalize the dinner in a "literary style." He is a generalized audience incarnate. In all this publicity, with Lily at the height of her social facility, Bertha announces that Lily is not going back to the yacht. Amid the general embarrassment, Selden longs to throw Dabham into the street. True to her training, Lily remains composed, stating that as she is joining the duchess the next day, it seems more convenient to stay the night on shore. After giving a tentative glance at the other women's faces and reading their incredulity, she turns to Selden "with an easy gesture, and the pale bravery of her recovered smile," saying that he had promised to see her to her cab. While Lily's poise and self-control in this scene lift her momentarily above her antagonist—reveal in fact her full magnificence—the role of proud independence she has chosen to play before witnesses passes inward, crystallizing her self-reliance and making it more difficult for her to seek or accept sympathy. Outside with Selden, she maintains her aloof dignity, choosing rather to mock his earlier advice about leaving the yacht than to explain or defend herself. Under public constraint she has chosen her role; in private she will play it out.

So powerful is the sense of an audience in Wharton's fiction that it becomes internalized. Even when alone, her protagonists carry with them an awareness of society's judgments; they seem to exist only in relationship to their community. It is the pressure of onlookers that transforms outward manners into laws of thought. Scrutinizing others and conscious of being scrutinized by them, the people in Wharton's fiction understandably elevate the conventions by which they judge and are judged into eternal moral principles. They develop a communal state of mind. The assumptions a character shares with his society bind him to that society, and in Wharton's fiction those assumptions take up a great deal of room in the characters' minds.

In her finest ritual scene, the Archers' farewell dinner for Ellen Olenska, Wharton brings together all the powers she sees in the formal gatherings of society. Archer recognizes that the congenial people eating May's canvasback duck and Florida asparagus are engaged in a silent conspiracy against himself and Ellen, whom they assume to be lovers. Their very cordiality expresses their relief at the fact that Ellen is leaving without "unpleasantness." Archer guesses that he himself has been "the centre of countless silently observing eyes and patiently listening ears." Somehow this quiet audience has effected his separation from Ellen and is now tacitly assuming that no one ever imagined any threat to Archer's marriage. Against such silences and implications one can raise no protest or defense, and Archer discovers the full power of New York's conventions for "taking life 'without effusion of blood':

the way of people who dreaded scandal more than disease, who placed decency above courage, and who considered that nothing was more ill-bred than scenes, except the behaviour of those who gave rise to them" (p. 338).

As propriety dictates that Madame Olenska, the guest of honor, must be seated at Archer's right, so the rules of formal dining decree that he must talk politely to her under surveillance, a responsibility recalled to him by May's quick glance down the table. Thus when Archer most wants to talk to Ellen in private, he must say only those things he could say to any guest. Chafing at this constraint, he asserts loudly that he means to do some traveling himself, and having made this plunge, he calls down the table to Reggie Chivers, proposing a trip around the world. But Reggie's wife reminds her husband that he cannot go before the Martha Washington ball, and after that Reggie himself will be practicing polo. Consequently, even this minor rebellion is quelled by conventional assumptions, and Archer's outburst ends in Mr. Selfridge Merry's circumstantial anecdotes about his own trip around the world.

After dinner the guests ally to keep Madame Olenska busy talking to everyone but Archer, and when she is ready to leave, the van der Luydens sweep her away in their landau, not even giving him the chance to take his final leave of her in private. The romance that has carried Archer into a larger world ends formally under the maximum constraint of a smaller world. Instead of sharing the communal mind, Archer finds himself judged and imprisoned by it. But under these restrictions his love for Ellen and the freer world she represents emerges more poignantly and convincingly than anywhere else in the novel.

And yet New York's assumptions continue to reverberate in Archer's mind. He cannot wholly escape his society; its witnesses govern his thoughts. When he most wants to be free, he most clearly recognizes the sanctions of his social order, and it is his own shrewd awareness of what lies behind the politeness of his guests that gives the dinner scene such great force. By understanding New York's rituals, Archer is obliged to acknowledge its judgments.

The Spirit Contained

The ritual assemblies in Wharton's fiction not only epitomize her ideas about manners and her procedures for dealing with them; they also objectify in dramatic form her vision of human experience, and thus they provide a useful focus for an assessment of her fiction. Her finest art incorporates a vision of containment, with the individual spirit making its nearly futile assertions in the midst of extraordinary constraint. In these formal gatherings the private narrative intersects the public one, and the forces of both sequences combine for the reader in an intense feeling of climax. But insofar as such scenes become major narrative climaxes, the implication is that private lines of intention culminate in public, and even the buried desires of the protagonists come to account before an assembled society. Whatever power or authority the protagonist recognizes in such a scene measures his personal complicity in the public ritual, as can be seen in the difference between Ellen's simple pleasure and Archer's grave embarrassment during the opening scene at the opera. That Wharton's public scenes have such narrative power suggests the severe limitations she imposes on the personal lives of her characters.

In contrast to the skills lying behind such vibrant narrative scenes as Cooper's initiation of Deerslayer into human warfare, Hawthorne's projection of Hester and Dimmesdale's midnight vigil on the scaffold, or Balzac's picture of Vautrin's arrest in *Père Goriot*, a novelist's ability to dramatize and intensify ritualistic social gatherings rests primarily on observation rather than on imagination. And it is in social observation, illuminated by urgent and searching questions about the effects of manners, that Edith Wharton engages her greatest strength as a novelist; she creates a substantial and comprehensible image of human beings as they live in society. While informing her narratives with acute and far-reaching generalizations, she represents human life in its particularities—the details and gestures from which moral theories must initially derive and to which they must ultimately apply. If she fails to give imaginative embodiment to self-responsible individuals, she succeeds admirably at showing her characters in their social relatedness and at making the spectacle serious and moving. Acting under surveillance and within codified forms, these characters learn to think, to perceive, and to judge as the assumptions and feelings of their communities dictate. Patterns of conduct become systems of thought and feeling. And in revealing the restraints manners impose, Wharton also affirms their underlying value for both social and personal coherence.

Her own work illustrates a principle she states in *A Backward Glance*—the value of a novelist's subject depends almost wholly on what he sees in it, and especially on how deeply he sees *into* it. Although her subject matter was narrow in its own time and is now socially remote as well, she brings to it the firm intelligence and the keen observation that can make forgotten customs matter. Her fiction is a persuasive account of how much human life is dominated by seeming trivialities, habits, inherited and unanalyzed assumptions; and she shows the extent to which our moral judgments depend on, and must account for, the codes of behavior in a specific social order. Rather than encourage us to entertain imaginative possibilities or wide ranges of feeling, Edith Wharton uses narrative as a subtle mode of inquiry, forcing us to take a hard look at the effects of social organization. Although outward manners prevail in her fiction too easily over inner resources, she dignifies personal loss by the very understanding it provides.

But in responding to Edith Wharton's fiction, one finds oneself too often measuring the inward dignity of outward defeat, the quiet gains that survive loss or renunciation, the spiritual enrichment of one who acquiesces in the inevitable. There is an evasion here that cannot be wholly attributed to her hard scrutiny of things as they are. As Wharton sublimates defeat, substitutes awareness of social complexity for assertion of personal imperatives, and forces her characters to civilize their passions, she evinces a cast of temperament that damages her art and her moral vision as well. One has, of course, the responsibility to acknowledge and to understand both one's social order and one's complex relation to it, and Wharton's fiction is a fine tribute to this responsibility. But one has another responsibility, perhaps most disconcertingly affirmed in the literature of prophecy, not to acquiesce too easily, not to accommodate oneself to the seemingly inevitable until one has asked *Why?* with all the energy of the other, less expressible feelings that prompt the spirit. Of this responsibility Wharton makes little acknowledgment; neither she nor, consequently, her protagonists can summon up the creative energy to imagine the self as existing in other realms than the social, as owing allegiance to other powers and ideals than those contained in the traditions of a community and the larger historical development of social groups. In an extreme form it is this kind of energy that allows Henry Thoreau, at least temporarily, to project a self quite outside the social container, looking in curiously, even impishly, and asking questions so audacious and yet so playful as to make the "inevitable" seem an impertinence.

One cannot, of course, ask of Edith Wharton that she employ Thoreau's imaginative and linguistic modes of exploring the self; her purposes are entirely different. But she represents an opposite extreme, and her inability to imagine the free self has serious consequences in her characterization. As she herself implies in her thorough study of perceptual fixations, the failure to conceive nonsocial beings carries with it an incapacity to recognize the full range of human possibilities. Her protagonists are not poorly drawn, nor are they incredible; they are simply incomplete. In terms of their passions, their assertions of will, their ideals and intuitions, they seem impotent. And this impotence is certainly not endemic to the novel of manners. Austen, Thackeray, Balzac, Tolstoy, and Proust, to name some of Wharton's favorite examples, project characters crucially defined by manners. But this is only one component of characterization, and there are others, equally natural, which give their protagonists that quality of human resistance so conspicuously missing in Wharton's characters.

Again, however, it seems more helpful to look at Edith Wharton in the context of American literature, for she is, curiously enough, as self-conscious about manners and social structures as Emerson or Mark Twain. There is an underlying discontent in her social observation, an incapacity to take one's social and historical connectedness for granted as simply one part of the self. In her constant urge to explain the network of manners and to assert its significance, one senses her fear that if manners really are important, they must be all-important. There is, after all, a germ of wisdom in the American preference for characters as against personages, in the suspicions about social definition shared by Emerson, Thoreau, Twain, James, Faulkner, and Fitzgerald. If it must be done with deliberate and self-conscious effort, the very process of delineating or understanding a personage dissipates one's personal energy in a complex analysis of social patterns. And whatever consumes so much of one's effort takes on all the force of a primary reality.

This process affects one's conception of moral issues as well, giving primacy to those aspects of conduct and feeling that are acknowledged in a community or in a historical tradition. Wharton's clear, firm elaboration of those moral issues involving the complex interlocking of class taboos and cultural sanctions stands in sharp contrast to one of the finest qualities of a major tradition in American literature. In such figures as Hester Prynne, Ishmael, the "I" of *Walden*, Leatherstocking, Huck Finn, Isabel Archer, Nick Adams, and especially Ike McCaslin, we see characters not so much rebelling against the complex imperatives of social experience as freed from them, groping their way tentatively, experimentally, often unwillingly, through their feelings and intuitions toward other imperatives, so broad, so simple, so commanding, so close to the heart, that they cannot be contained in the verbal forms made accessible by social experience and cannot be resisted, despite all the temptations to acquiesce in the seemingly inevitable.

For all Edith Wharton's intelligence about manners and their effects, then, her fiction suffers from the absence of other kinds of intelligence, other imaginative resources. And this fact matters not only in assessing Wharton's limitations as a novelist but also in coming to terms with what it means to read and understand her fiction. For the art of narrative has wonderful and strange capacities to implicate the reader. In dealing with plot structure, with immediate representation of manners, and with prose style, I described some of the specific ways in which Wharton's procedures force us into subtle complicities; here I am concerned with more general effects. In our very capacity to engage the right interests, to follow a story, especially among such complex issues and expectations as move Wharton's narratives, we are deeply implicated in the story itself. Thus in following Wharton's stories, we too disperse our energies and expectancies over a network of social complications, implicitly recognizing the overwhelming significance of manners for our own judgments and holding in abeyance or even forgetting our own capacities to step outside a socially circumscribed world.

Furthermore, narratives present us with images that have incalculable powers over our inner lives—they create people, and they show how life can be lived or at least imagined. By projecting and affirming certain possibilities of action, feeling, and posture, of nobility and degradation, they awaken in us echoes of our own latent capacities, even the socially portentous powers to dream and to wish. No matter how harshly we judge them or how little we may desire to imitate them, Captain Ahab and Madame Bovary enlarge our humanity. In this regard Edith Wharton's fiction presents us with forceful images of human life as contained and shaped by social habits. During our immersion in the network of manners, our awe at social power, we are given no compensatory images of the human spirit asserting itself in implacable, even if futile, resistance. We are affirmed in our weakness, shown that our limitations are inevitable, that genuine resistance to them only denies the roots of our personality. And by implicitly sharing Wharton's sense of vast, slow historical changes and seeing nobility only in the act of sublimating personal defeat by referring it to this larger movement, we are temporarily incapacitated to look about us and, as Melville puts it, to say NO! in thunder.

Yet there is value in the reminder of our containment. In the context of a literature often engaged in flights to the intuitive sublime, it is a useful antidote to confront a lucid, probing examination of life at the daily level. In juxtaposition with Edith Wharton's best fiction, Emerson seems a bit foolish and Henry James rarefied. And as Edith Wharton forces us to recognize the seriousness of manners, she also inadvertently confirms many of our suspicions about them. What do the van der Luydens matter to us? More than we care and perhaps more than we ought to acknowledge.

Bibliographical Essay
and
Index

Bibliographical Essay

The body of criticism dealing with Edith Wharton's fiction has developed neither the range of inquiry nor the strength of judgment that the fiction itself deserves. For a writer so problematic, so contradictory and disturbing as Wharton, much of the criticism is surprisingly superficial or peripheral, especially in assessing her serious limitations. Thus, rather than attempt to provide a thorough bibliography, I wish here to indicate what seem to me the most useful and suggestive essays or books, and in the process to acknowledge my own general indebtedness to a few of these. For an overall bibliography of Edith Wharton's writings and the criticism of them (through 1965), see Vito J. Brenni, *Edith Wharton: A Bibliography* (Morgantown, W.Va., 1966).

Until the completion of the biography incorporating the collection of papers recently opened at Yale, the materials for serious biographical analysis of Wharton's work will remain sketchy. But there are four important sources of information. The first and most obvious is her own autobiography, *A Backward Glance* (New York, 1934). Although this book is reticent, Wharton's reticence itself and her choices of what to tell about her life are valuable indicators of her personality and interests. *A Backward Glance* deserves a more serious investigation as an autobiography than it has yet had. Percy Lubbock's *Portrait of Edith Wharton* (London, 1947) was written by one of her close friends and includes personal memories from several other friends. Although this book is even less detailed than the autobiography, there are many fleeting but valuable suggestions in the often divergent anecdotes told by the people who knew her. But whereas *A Backward Glance* emphasizes the social, intellectual, and cultural backgrounds, the persons and forces that shaped Wharton's thought and feeling, Lubbock's *Portrait* omits the background entirely and dwells instead on the impressions she created among friends and strangers, especially in her later years in Europe. Wayne Andrews's Introduction to *The Best Short Stories of Edith Wharton* (New York, 1958) is the most useful brief summary of her life. It is more comprehensive and detailed than Lubbock's *Portrait*, and it introduces excerpts from her journals. Finally, Millicent Bell in *Edith Wharton and Henry James: The Story of·Their Friendship* (New York, 1965) adds many insights derived from letters to or about Wharton, especially from James. Her book is even more valuable, however, for seriously challenging the assumption that Wharton was Henry James's disciple. She discriminates justly between their characteristic interests and shows in some detail how differently they handled similar subjects.

The best overall examination of Wharton's writing is Blake Nevius's *Edith Wharton: A Study of Her Fiction* (Berkeley and Los Angeles, 1953). Its basic value lies in its range and comprehensiveness, its genetic examination of all parts of a long and diversified career, coupled with careful attention to Wharton's relationships to other writers, especially Balzac, George Eliot, and the literary naturalists. Nevius suggests the variety of interests that can be brought fruitfully to her fiction, and his book is virtually the starting point for serious criticism of her work. Two of his theoretical chapters are especially helpful. One deals with the theme of "the trapped spirit"—the larger nature caught up in the smaller one, as in the case of Ralph Marvell and Undine Spragg. The other, "Toward the Novel of Manners," provides a fine summary of the meaning and use of manners for Edith Wharton. Although Nevius deals with manners primarily as means of expression or differentiation (that is, as tools of the novelist) rather than as the determiners of personal perception, his definitions opened up some of the underlying conceptions of my own study of manners. The limitations of Nevius's study follow from its strengths; the very range of his inquiry prevents thorough scrutiny of the best novels, and in the case of *The House of Mirth* he seriously underestimates the character of Lily Bart.

The diversity of approaches and judgments in criticism about Edith Wharton is indicated in Irving Howe's *Edith Wharton: A Collection of Critical Essays* (Englewood Cliffs, N.J., 1962) for the Twentieth Century Views series. Howe's collection not only gathers most of the best essays before 1962, but it illustrates the absence of firm lines of inquiry and the baffling uncertainties of judgment that emerge when several studies are compared. Are the New England country people in *Ethan Frome* and *Summer* evidence of Wharton's range of observation and imaginative sympathy, or do they illustrate her failure to reach outside her own class background? Is *The Reef* one of her best novels because it shows James's influence, or does its only genuine interest lie in showing this influence? For those critics concerned with Wharton's affinities to James, *The Reef* assumes an importance out of line with its intrinsic interest or merit. It is, in fact, the least characteristic of her longer fictions.

But there are other approaches in Howe's collection, essays that attempt to locate the distinctive properties of Edith Wharton's fiction. Edmund Wilson's "Justice to Edith Wharton" (1941) not only suggests the power of the personal maladjustments that motivate her stories but focuses attention on her protagonists as "victims of the group pressure of convention," imaginative spirits locked in a closed system. Lionel Trilling's essay on *Ethan Frome*, "The Morality of Inertia" (1956), elucidates a theme that appears in much of Wharton's major fiction: "that moral inertia, the *not* making of moral decisions, constitutes a large part of the moral life of humanity." He sees her characters as having no strength to refuse unspoken social demands or even to imagine refusing, and he judges her harshly for creating such cruel situations with so little moral reverberation. Trilling's strictures are serious enough to merit close consideration; I have tried to account for his thesis in discussing Wharton's examination of moral life at "the daily level." Irving Howe's "Introduction: The Achievement of Edith Wharton" is an extremely useful brief assessment of her fiction. I have followed out some of his major theses: that she had an overdeveloped sense of the social powers that check our desires; that she sees society as a prison of the soul and yet examines it with the cool spirit of an anthropologist; that she never achieved James's sense of individual transcendence, his ability to embody convincing images of the human will resisting defeat.

The best specific analyses of Wharton's novels have dealt with *The House of Mirth*, and some of the overall directions of my own study were indicated in four essays. Two are included in Howe's collection, his own Introduction to the Rinehart edition of *The*

House of Mirth (New York, 1962) and Diana Trilling's "*The House of Mirth* Revisited" (1947; revised). Howe's essay focuses on the conflict between Lily's acquired taste for luxury and her natural taste for refinement, an example of the larger problem of mediating between the expectations of commercial society and the ideals of civilization. He sees the moral positives as disembodied in the novel, as surviving only in terms of their violation, and he points out that even the moral standards of New Yorkers serve as strategies of exclusion rather than as guides to conduct. In a world of steady calculation, he finds Wharton especially concerned with the personal cost of genuine emotion. Mrs. Trilling focuses on the subtle bonds between social realities and the emotional life. She sees Wharton's distinctive value in her particularization of society, her stance within the socially given. From this stance she can recognize the ways in which Lily is tainted by her environment and measure society's toll in its defeat of feeling. Mrs. Trilling sees the book as developing the complex interplay between the personal destiny and that decreed by a particular social situation.

Two other essays on *The House of Mirth* that were especially helpful to me have appeared since Howe's collection: R. W. B. Lewis's Introduction to the Riverside edition of *The House of Mirth* (Boston, 1963) and the chapter "Panoramic Environment and the Anonymity of the Self," in Richard Poirier's *A World Elsewhere: The Place of Style in American Literature* (New York, 1966). Lewis clearly establishes the degree to which society lies at the center of Wharton's fiction as a thing apart from the characters, a third party to their personal encounters, and he sees the action of the book as having its locus in a segment of social history. In the formal discrepancy between books 1 and 2, Lewis finds Wharton virtually inventing a genre to convey what is happening socially: the House of Mirth, with its own kind of drama, is giving way to other houses. In fact, Wharton's fiction involves for Lewis a drama of place, an organic interplay between buildings and psyches. His analysis of the social transitions underlying the book also accounts in a crucial way for the ineffectuality of Wharton's seemingly sympathetic figures like Lawrence Selden: when social change dislocates manners and morals by gradually severing the actual from the ideal, not only do everyday manners become cruder, but the ideal itself and the characters who cling to it become bloodless by their divorce from the actual. Poirier also focuses his attention on Wharton's representation of society; he points out her difficulties in giving dramatic embodiment within the dominant forces of her world to her own values of intimacy and human solidarity. In a society in which emotions, like money, are calculated and invested, there is no place for the sustained expression of uncalculated feeling, nor are there even modes of action or expression by which one's best impulses could be revealed. Society becomes for Wharton an expression of impersonal power, and Poirier sees her surrendering her interest to the environmental powers that forbid personal fulfillment.

Three other essays are valuable for suggesting Wharton's place among novelists and critics of American society: Frederick Hoffmann, "Points of Moral Reference: A Comparative Study of Edith Wharton and F. Scott Fitzgerald," in *English Institute Essays, 1949* (New York, 1950); Christof Wegelin, "Edith Wharton and the Twilight of the International Novel," *Southern Review,* N.S. 5 (1969), 398-418; and the chapter "Edith Wharton and the Realists," in D. E. S. Maxwell's *American Fiction* (New York, 1963). Hoffmann traces Wharton's advantages in having a fixed point of reference in the stable social ideals she projects as underlying old New York. From this moral perspective she can plot the sins and complexities of a world that is falling away; by not shifting her stance in response to social change, she maintains a confident critical view of an unstable world. Wegelin's study traces the shifting lines of cultural contrast in the development of the "international novel," and this context allows him to locate many distinctive features of *The Custom of the Country.* Maxwell's excellent essay examines *The House of Mirth, The Custom of the Country,* and *The Age of Innocence* in the context of historical, social, and intellectual changes in America. Resisting the common tendency to regard Wharton as a novelist divorced from the exigencies of her own country, he places her firmly in a tradition of American novelists dealing with the crucial issues of American society. In particular he traces her relationship to William Graham Sumner's thesis (which consolidated widespread attitudes at the turn of the century) that the individual's only profitable function is to conform to the social mores that have educated him. Maxwell sees Wharton as showing the suffocating paramountcy of this ethic in relationships of personal intimacy. In Lily Bart she projects the possibility of resisting contemporary mores in the name of higher loyalties. In *The Custom of the Country* she assesses the failure of the old order to transmit its traditions as a living organism to the new generation. And in *The Age of Innocence* she probes the weaknesses of a class that deliberately divorced itself from the legal and political forces of its time and found even its business power growing irrelevant. As Wharton represents current social forms, then, Maxwell sees her as exploring the core of beliefs underlying them; she penetrates social paraphernalia to reveal the moral diversity of that segment of America she knew best.

Index

Adams, Henry, 40
Age of Innocence, The, 1, 9, 10, 11, 41, 48-49, 52-53, 76-86, 100-108, 110, 112-14, 128-37, 147-48, 151-57, 162, 164, 167, 169-70
Andrews, Wayne, 180
Auerbach, Erich, 37
Austen, Jane, 1, 3, 18, 138, 144-45, 164

Babb, Howard S., 144*n*
Backward Glance, A, 7, 37, 51, 179
Balzac, Honoré de, 1, 3, 13, 21, 36, 48*n*, 72, 124
Père Goriot, 31, 70, 161-62
Bell, Millicent, 180
Bewley, Marius, 20*n*
Brenni, Vito J., 179
Buccaneers, The, 10, 111

Chase, Richard, 20*n*
Clemens, Samuel L. [pseud. Mark Twain], 173
Coleridge, Samuel Taylor, 39
Conrad, Joseph, 47
Cooper, James Fenimore, 1, 18, 20-22, 25
Croll, Morris, 149
Custom of the Country, The, 10, 11, 48, 50-51, 57, 67-76, 93-100, 110, 111, 114, 115-22, 145-47, 162-63, 166, 167

Dreiser, Theodore, 34
Durkheim, Émile, 14-15

Eastlake, Charles, 103
Eliot, George, 13, 18, 36, 85*n*
Middlemarch, 15, 19, 157-59
Emerson, Ralph Waldo, 26-27, 33, 36, 39, 173
Ethan Frome, 10, 50, 181

Faulkner, William, 47
Fitzgerald, F. Scott, 1, 4, 26, 30, 33-34, 36, 173
Flaubert, Gustave, 13, 47
Madame Bovary, 16-17, 19
Fruit of the Tree, The, 38, 85*n*, 111, 146-47

Girard, René, 97-98
Glasgow, Ellen, 34
Glimpses of the Moon, 11, 142
Gods Arrive, The, 39

Hardy, Barbara, 2*n*, 43*n*
Hawthorne, Nathaniel: *The Scarlet Letter,* 81, 165
Hoffmann, Frederick, 183
Houghton, Walter, 17
House of Mirth, The, 10, 11, 46, 48, 54, 56-57, 61-67, 77, 82, 87-93, 112, 122-28, 141, 142-45, 168-69
Howe, Irving, 180, 181-82
Howells, William Dean, 4, 18, 20-21, 22-23, 24, 25, 34, 36, 72
The Rise of Silas Lapham, 23-24, 70

James, Henry, 1, 13, 20*n*, 26, 27, 34, 36, 42, 47, 165-66, 173
The Europeans, 24
The Portrait of a Lady, 19, 27-33, 128, 157-59

Lewis, R. W. B., 25*n*, 35, 182-83
Lubbock, Percy, 179

Manners: defined, 3
Mark Twain. *See* Clemens, Samuel L.
Maxwell, D. E. S., 183-84
"Mortal Lease, The," 40-41

Nevius, Blake, 52*n*, 85*n*, 180
New Year's Day, 113
Novel of manners: defined, 1-4; relation
    to context of romanticism, 13-14, 19;
    images of society and self in American
    novels of manners, 19-34

Ohmann, Richard M., 140*n*

Parrington, Vernon L., 1
Poirier, Richard, 20*n*, 33*n*, 34-35, 182,
    183
Poulet, Georges, 48*n*
Proust, Marcel, 47

Reef, The, 10, 85*n*, 181
Rossetti, Dante Gabriel, 133

Shroder, Maurice Z., 2*n*
Son at the Front, A, 39
Stendhal [Marie Henri Beyle], 36, 72
    The Red and the Black, 15, 31, 70,
    161
Stoicism, 149
Summer, 10, 181
Sumner, William Graham, 183

Thackeray, William M., 36, 164
Thoreau, Henry David, 26, 173
Tocqueville, Alexis de, 20
Tolstoy, Leo, 163-64
Trilling, Diana, 182
Trilling, Lionel, 3*n*, 19, 20*n*, 181
Tuttleton, James W., 20*n*
Twilight Sleep, 11

Valley of Decision, The, 10, 15-16, 41-
    42, 59, 117, 150
Van Ghent, Dorothy, 32

Wegelin, Christof, 183
Westermarck, Edward, 7-8*n*
Wharton, Edith: general summary of
    subject matter, 4-10; interest in an-
    thropology, 7-10; attitudes toward
    self and society, 34-42; description
    of her plotting, 44-60; fable of rescue
    in her fiction, 45-46, 55-60; manners
    and perception in her characteriza-
    tion, 51-55
Wilson, Edmund, 181
Winner, Viola Hopkins, 153-54
Writing of Fiction, The, 31, 109, 139

Zola, Émile, 48*n*

R3